UNDERSTANDING THE BIBLE

By the same author:

UNDERSTANDING THE BIBLE

by John R. W. Stott

Published in Great Britain by
Scripture Union
5 Wigmore Street, London W1H OAD

Published in the United States by
Regal Books Division, G/L Publications
Glendale, California 91209   U.S.A.

© John Stott 1972
First published 1972
Reprinted 1972
Reprinted 1973

Library of Congress Catalog Card No. 72–77801
ISBN 0 85421 327 9

Illustrations by Annie Vallatton
Maps by Liz Leyland

Printed in Great Britain by
Hazell Watson & Viney Ltd, Aylesbury, Bucks

CONTENTS

LIST OF MAPS

PREFACE

Every author owes it to the reading public to explain himself. Why has he thought fit to swell the torrent of books—especially religious books—which pours from the world's printing presses every day? Can he justify his rash enterprise? Let me at least tell you frankly the kind of people I have had in mind while writing. They fall into two categories.

First, the new Christian. With the spread of secularism in our day, an increasing number of people are being added to Christ and His Church who have no religious background whatever. Here, for example, is a young man from a non-Christian family. The Christian instruction he received at school was minimal, and possibly misleading. In any case the fashion was to pay no attention to it. He did not go to Sunday School as a kid, and he has seldom if ever been to church. But now he has found Christ, or rather been found by Him. He is told he must read the Bible daily if he is to grow into spiritual maturity. The Bible is a closed book to him, however— an unexplored, uncharted territory. Who wrote it, he asks, and when, where and why? What is its message? What is the foundation for its claim to be a 'holy' or special book, the book of God? And how is it to be read and interpreted? These are proper questions to ask, and some answer must be given to them before the new Christian can derive maximum benefit from his Bible reading.

Then, secondly, there is the Christian of several years' standing. In the main, he has been a conscientious Bible reader. He has read his portion faithfully every day. But somehow it has become a stale habit. The years have passed, and he himself has changed and matured as a person. Yet he has not developed as a Christian in any comparable way. A sign (and cause) of this is that he still reads the Bible as he did when he was a child, or a new convert. Now he is tired of his superficiality, his immaturity, and not a little ashamed. He longs to become an adult, integrated Christian, who knows and pleases God, fulfils himself in serving others and can commend the gospel in meaningful terms to a lost, bewildered generation.

My desire is to assure such a Christian that the secrets of Christian maturity are ready to be found in Scripture by all who seek them. There is a breadth to God's Word which few of us ever encompass, a depth which we seldom plumb.

In particular, our Christianity is mean because our Christ is mean. We impoverish ourselves by our low and paltry views of Him. Some speak of Him today as if He were a kind of syringe to be carried about in our pocket, so that when we are feeling depressed we can give ourselves a fix and take a trip into fantasy. But Christ cannot be used or manipulated like that. The contemporary Church seems to have little understanding of the greatness of Jesus Christ as lord of creation and lord of the Church, before whom our place is on our faces in the dust. Nor do we seem to see His victory as the New Testament portrays it, with all things under His feet, so that if we are joined to Christ, all things are under our feet as well.

It seems to me that our greatest need today is an enlarged vision of Jesus Christ. We need to see Him as the One in whom alone the fulness of God dwells and in whom alone we can come to fulness of life.[1]

There is only one way to gain clear, true, fresh, lofty views of Christ, and that is through the Bible. The Bible is the prism by which the light of Jesus Christ is broken into its many and beautiful colours. The Bible is the portrait of Jesus Christ. We need to gaze upon Him with such intensity of desire that (by the gracious work of the Holy Spirit) He comes alive to us, meets with us, and fills us with Himself.

In order to apprehend Jesus Christ in His fulness, it is essential to understand the setting within which God offers Him to us. God gave Christ to the world in a specific geographical, historical and theological context. More simply, He sent Him to a particular place (Palestine), at a particular time (the climax of centuries of Jewish history) and within a particular framework of truth (progressively revealed and permanently recorded in the Bible). So the following chapters are concerned with the geography, history, theology, authority and interpretation of the Bible. Their object is to present the setting within which God once revealed and now offers Christ, so that we may the better grasp for ourselves and share with others the glorious fulness of Jesus Christ Himself.

NOTE

1 See Col. 1.19; 2.9, 10

1. THE PURPOSE OF THE BIBLE

The choice of a book to read and the way in which we read it are determined largely by the author's purpose in writing it. Is it a textbook of science or history intended to inform, or a novel meant purely to entertain? Is it a piece of serious prose or poetry in which the writer reflects on life and stimulates the reader to think about it too? Does it speak in any meaningful way to the contemporary world? Or is it perhaps a controversial work in which he deliberately sets out to argue his point of view? Moreover, is the author qualified to write on his subject? It is questions like these which are in our minds when we ask 'Is it worth reading?'

Most books supply the prospective reader with the information he wants about who wrote them and why. Either the author tells us candidly in a Preface about himself and his object in writing, or the publisher does so in the 'blurb' on the dust cover. Most readers spend time examining these before committing themselves to buy, borrow or read the book.

It is a great pity that readers of the Bible do not always pursue the same enquiries. Many appear to pick it up and begin their reading at random. Or they start at Genesis and get stuck in Leviticus. Or they may doggedly persevere from a sense of duty, even reading the whole Bible through section by section in five years, but without deriving much benefit from their study because they lack understanding of the book's overall purpose. Or indeed they may give up Bible reading, or never start it, because they cannot see how the tale of a far-away people in a far-away age could have any relevance for them today.

In any case, how can the Bible, which in fact is not a book but a library of sixty-six books, possibly be said to have a 'purpose'? Was it not compiled by different authors at different times with different objectives? Yes and no. There is indeed a wide variety of human author and theme. Yet behind these, Christians believe, there lies a single divine Author with a single unifying theme.

What this theme is the Bible itself declares. It is stated several times in several places, but perhaps nowhere more succinctly than by the Apostle Paul to Timothy:

'From childhood you have been acquainted with the sacred writings which are able to instruct you for salvation through faith in Christ Jesus. All Scripture is inspired by God and profitable for teaching, for reproof, for correction, and for training in righteousness, that the man of God may be complete, equipped for every good work.'[1]

Here the apostle brings together both the origin and the object of Scripture, where it comes from and what it is intended for. Its origin: 'inspired by God'. Its object: 'profitable' for men. Indeed, it is profitable for men only because it is inspired by God. The subject of Biblical inspiration I must leave to a later chapter; in this chapter I want to investigate the nature of the Bible's profitability. For this I will take up three words which Paul used— 'salvation', 'Christ' and 'faith'.

A Book of Salvation

Perhaps no Biblical word has suffered more from misuse and misunderstanding than the word 'salvation'. Some of us Christians are to blame for the caricature of it which we have presented to the world. As a result, 'salvation' has become for many a source of embarrassment, even an object of ridicule. We need to rescue it from the narrow concept to which we have often debased it. For 'salvation' is a big and noble word, as I shall soon elaborate. Salvation is freedom. Yes, and renewal too; ultimately the renewal of the whole cosmos.

Now the supreme purpose of the Bible, Paul writes to Timothy, is to instruct its readers 'for salvation'. This immediately indicates that Scripture has a practical purpose, and that this purpose is moral rather than intellectual. Or rather its intellectual instruction (its 'wisdom', as the Greek word implies) is given with a view to the moral experience called 'salvation'.

In order to grasp more firmly this positive purpose of Scripture, it may be helpful to contrast it with some negatives.

First, the purpose of the Bible is not scientific. This is not to say that the teaching of Scripture and of science are in conflict with one another for, when we keep each to its proper sphere, they are not. Indeed, if the God of truth is the author of both, they could not be. Nor is it to say that the two spheres never overlap and that nothing in the Bible partakes of the nature of science, for the Bible does contain statements of fact which can be (and in many cases have been) scientifically verified. For example, a number of historical facts are recorded, such as that Nebuchadrezzar King of Babylon besieged, took and virtually destroyed Jerusalem, and that Jesus of Nazareth was born when Augustus was Emperor of Rome. What I am rather asserting is that, though the Bible may contain some science, the *purpose* of the Bible is not scientific.

Science (or at least natural science) is a body of knowledge painstakingly acquired by observation, experiment and induction. The purpose of God through Scripture, however, has been to disclose truths which could not be discovered by this empirical method, but would have remained unknown and undiscovered if He had not revealed them. For instance, science may be able to tell us something about man's physical origins (even this is an open question); only the Bible reveals man's nature, both his unique nobility as a creature made in the Creator's image and his degradation as a self-centred sinner in revolt against his Creator.

Next, the purpose of the Bible is not literary. Some years ago a book was published entitled *The Bible Designed to be read as Literature*. It was beautifully produced. Versification was abandoned. And the lay-out indicated plainly what was poetry and what prose. All this was helpful. Further, no one can deny, whatever his beliefs or disbeliefs, that the Bible does contain noble literature. It treats the great themes of human life and destiny, and handles them with simplicity, insight and imagination. So fine is the translation in some countries that the Bible has become part of the nation's literary heritage. Nevertheless, God did not design the Bible as great literature. It contains some glaring stylistic weaknesses. The New Testament was largely written in *koine* Greek, the everyday language of market and office, and much of it lacks literary polish, even grammatical accuracy. The purpose of the Bible is to be found in its message, not its style.

14

Thirdly, the purpose of the Bible is not philosophical. Of course Scripture contains profound wisdom, in fact the wisdom of God. But some of the great themes with which philosophers have always wrestled are not given a thorough treatment in Scripture. Take the great problems of suffering and evil. As phenomena of human experience they figure prominently throughout the Bible. On almost every page men sin and men suffer. And some light is thrown—supremely by the cross—on both problems. But no ultimate solution to either is offered, nor are the ways of God justified in relation to them. Even in the Book of Job, which concentrates on the problem of suffering, Job in the end humbles himself before God without understanding God's providence. I think the reason is simply that the Bible is more a practical than a theoretical book. It is more concerned to tell us how to bear suffering and overcome evil than it is to philosophize about their origin and purpose.

So the Bible is primarily a book neither of science, nor of literature, nor of philosophy, but of salvation.

In saying this we must give the word 'salvation' its broadest possible meaning. Salvation is far more than the forgiveness of sins. It includes the whole sweep of God's purpose to redeem and restore mankind, and indeed all creation. What we claim for the Bible is that it unfolds God's total plan.

It begins with the creation, so that we may know the divine likeness in which we were made, the obligations which we have repudiated and the heights from which we have fallen. We can understand neither what we are in sin nor what we may be by grace until we know what we once were by creation.

The Bible goes on to tell us how sin entered into the world, and death as a result of sin. It emphasizes the gravity of sin as a revolt against the authority of God our Creator and Lord, and the justice of His judgment upon

15

it. There are many salutary warnings in Scripture about the perils of disobedience.

But the main thrust of the Biblical message, as will be elaborated in chapter 5, is that God loves the very rebels who deserve nothing at His hand but judgment. Before time began, Scripture says, His plan of salvation took shape. It originated in His grace, His free and unmerited mercy. He made with Abraham a covenant of grace, promising through his posterity to bless all the families of the earth. The rest of the Old Testament is devoted to an account of His gracious dealings with Abraham's posterity, the people of Israel. In spite of their obstinate rejection of His word, as it came to them through law and prophets, He never cast them off. *They* broke the covenant, not He.

The historical coming of Jesus Christ was in fulfilment of His covenant:

'Blessed be the Lord God of Israel,
for He has visited and redeemed His people,
and has raised up a horn of salvation for us
in the house of His servant David,
as He spoke by the mouth of His holy prophets
    from of old,
that we should be saved from our enemies,
and from the hand of all who hate us;
to perform the mercy promised to our fathers,
and to remember His holy covenant,
the oath which He swore to our father Abraham, to
    grant us
that we, being delivered from the hand of our enemies,
might serve Him without fear,
in holiness and righteousness before Him all the days
    of our life.'[2]

It is important to observe that the promised 'salvation' from 'our enemies' is understood in terms of 'holiness and righteousness' and—later in the *Benedictus*—of 'the forgiveness of their sins through the tender mercy of our God'.

So the New Testament concentrates on the outworking of this salvation, on the way of 'forgiveness' and of 'holiness' through Jesus Christ's death, resurrection and gift of the Spirit. The apostles emphasize that forgiveness is possible only through the sin-bearing death of Christ, and a new birth leading to a new life only through the Spirit of Christ. Then the epistles are full of practical ethical instruction. As the NEB renders 2 Timothy 3.16, Scripture is profitable not only 'for teaching the truth and refuting error' but 'for reformation of manners and discipline in right living'. It also portrays Christ's Church as the society of the saved, who are called to a life of sacrificial service and witness in the world.

Finally, the New Testament authors insist that although God's people have already in one sense been saved, in another their salvation lies still in the future. We are given the promise that one day our bodies will be redeemed. 'In this hope we were saved.'[3] And in this final redemption the whole creation will somehow be involved. If we are to be clothed with new bodies, there is also going to be a new heaven and a new earth pervaded by righteousness alone. Then and only then, with no sin either in our nature or in our society, will God's salvation be complete. The glorious liberty of God's children will be the freedom to serve. God will be everything to everybody.[4]

Such is the comprehensive salvation set forth in Scripture. Conceived in a past eternity, achieved at a point in time and historically worked out in human experience, it will reach its consummation in the eternity of the future. The Bible is unique in its claim to instruct us for 'such a great salvation.'[5]

17

The salvation for which the Bible instructs us is available 'through faith in Christ Jesus'. Therefore, since Scripture concerns salvation and salvation is through Christ, Scripture is full of Christ.

Jesus Himself thus understood the nature and function of the Bible. 'The Scriptures,' He said, 'bear witness to Me.'[6] Again, walking with two disciples after the Resurrection from Jerusalem to Emmaus, He rebuked them for their folly and unbelief, due to their ignorance of Scripture. Luke who tells the story adds:

'And beginning with Moses and all the prophets, He interpreted to them in all the scriptures the things concerning Himself.'[7]

A little while later the risen Lord said to a wider group of His followers:

'These are My words which I spoke to you, while I was still with you, that everything written about Me in the law of Moses and the prophets and the psalms must be fulfilled.'[8]

Christ's assertion was, then, not only that the Scriptures bore witness to Him in a general way but that in each of the three divisions of Old Testament Scripture—the law, the prophets and the psalms (or 'writings')—there were things concerning Him, and that all these things must be fulfilled.

The fundamental relation between the Old Testament and the New Testament, according to Christ, is that between promise and fulfilment. The very first word Jesus uttered in His public ministry (in the Greek text of the Gospel of Mark) indicates this. It was the word 'fulfilled':

'The time is fulfilled, and the kingdom of God is at hand; repent, and believe in the gospel.'[9]

Jesus Christ was deeply convinced that the long centuries of expectation were over, and that He Himself had ushered in the days of fulfilment. So He could say to His apostles:

'Blessed are your eyes, for they see, and your ears, for they hear. Truly, I say to you, many prophets and righteous men longed to see what you see, and did not see it, and to hear what you hear, and did not hear it.'[10]

In the light of this claim, we shall look first at the Old Testament in its three divisions, then at the New Testament, and try to see how our Saviour Jesus Christ Himself (in terms of promise and fulfilment) is Scripture's uniting theme.

By the 'law' was meant the Pentateuch, the first five books of the Old Testament. Can we really find Christ in them? Yes indeed.

To begin with, they contain some foundation prophecies of God's salvation through Christ, which underlie the rest of the Bible. God promised first that the seed of Eve would bruise the serpent's head, next that through Abraham's posterity He would bless all the families of the earth, and later that 'the sceptre shall not depart from Judah ... until He comes to whom it belongs', whom the people will obey.[11] Thus it was revealed—already in the first book of the Bible—that the Messiah would be human (descended from Eve) and Jewish (descended from Abraham and of the tribe of Judah), and that He would crush Satan, bless the world and rule as king for ever.

Another important prophecy of Christ in the law represents Him as being Himself the perfect Prophet. Moses said to the people:

19

'The Lord your God will raise up for you a Prophet like me from among you, from your brethren—Him you shall heed— . . . and I will put My words in His mouth, and He shall speak to them all that I command Him'.[12]

It was not only by direct prophecies that the law pointed forward to Christ, but also by more indirect pictures. In it the Messiah was foreshadowed as well as foretold. Indeed, God's dealings with Israel in choosing them, redeeming them, establishing His covenant with them, making atonement for their sins through sacrifice, and causing them to inherit the land of Canaan all set forth in limited and national terms what would one day be available to all men through Christ. Christians can say today: God has chosen us in Christ and made us a people for His own possession. Christ shed His blood to atone for our sins and ratify the new covenant. He has redeemed us not from Egyptian bondage but from the bondage of sin. He is our great high priest who offered Himself on the cross, as one sacrifice for sins for ever, and all priesthood and sacrifice are fulfilled in Him. Further, by His resurrection we have been born again to a living hope, 'to an inheritance which is imperishable, undefiled and unfading' and is reserved in heaven for us.[13] These great Christian words, which portray various aspects of our salvation through Christ—election, atonement, covenant, redemption, sacrifice, inheritance—all began to be used in the Old Testament of God's grace towards Israel.

There is yet a third way in which the law bears witness to Christ. It is elaborated by the apostle Paul in his Galatian letter:

'Now before faith came, we were confined under the law, kept under restraint until faith should be revealed. So that the law was our custodian until Christ came, that we might be justified by faith.'[14]

The law is vividly portrayed by the Greek words Paul used as a military garrison hemming us in ('confined'), a gaoler keeping us under lock and key ('under restraint') and a tutor charged with the discipline of minors ('our custodian'). All this is because the moral law condemned the lawbreaker without in itself offering any remedy. In this way it pointed to Christ. Its very condemnation made Christ necessary. It held us in bondage 'until Christ came', who alone could set us free. We are condemned by the law, but justified through faith in Christ.

Christ in the Prophets

As we turn now from the law to the prophets, we need to remember that the Old Testament division known as 'the prophets' included the history books (Joshua, Judges, Samuel and Kings) as 'the former prophets' because the authors were judged to have written prophetic or sacred history, as well as 'the latter prophets' whom we call the major and minor prophets.

Many readers of the Bible have found the history of Israel extremely tedious and cannot imagine how all those dreary kings could have anything to do with Christ! When we remember, however, that Christ's first words about 'the time is fulfilled' immediately led on to 'the kingdom of God has drawn near', we have in the word 'kingdom' the clue we need. Israel began as a 'theocracy', a nation under the direct rule of God. Even when the people rejected the divine rule by demanding a king like the other nations and God granted their request, they knew that ultimately He continued to be their King, for they continued to be His people, and that their kings reigned as it were as His viceroys.

Nevertheless, the rule of the kings, of both the northern kingdom Israel and the southern kingdom Judah, left much to be desired. The monarchy was marred now

21

externally by foreign wars, now internally by injustice and oppression. Both kingdoms also had the instability of all human institutions, as kings acceded to the throne and prospered and died. And sometimes they shrank to tiny territories as their land was overrun by invading armies, until in the end both capitals were taken and both nations suffered a humiliating exile. It is not surprising that God used their experience of the unsatisfactoriness of human rule to clarify their understanding of the perfections of the future Messianic kingdom and to strengthen their longing for it.

Already God had made a covenant with King David to build him a house and through his posterity to establish his throne for ever.[15] Now the prophets began to describe what kind of king this 'son of David' would be. They were clear that He would embody the ideals of kingship which the kings of Israel and Judah, and even David himself, so imperfectly foreshadowed. In His kingdom oppression would give place to justice, and war to peace. And there would be no limit to either its extent or its duration. For His dominion would stretch from sea to sea, even to the ends of the earth, and would last for ever. These four characteristics of the kingdom of the Messiah —peace, justice, universality and eternity—are brought together in one of Isaiah's most famous prophecies:

'For unto us a child is born, to us a son is given;
  and the government will be upon His shoulder, and His name will be called
  "Wonderful Counsellor, Mighty God, Everlasting Father, Prince of Peace."
  Of the increase of his government and of peace there will be no end,
  upon the throne of David, and over His kingdom,
    to establish it, and to uphold it
  with justice and with righteousness

from this time forth and for evermore.
The zeal of the Lord of hosts will do this.'[16]

If the prophets foretold the glory of the Messiah, they foretold His sufferings also. The best-known such prophecy, obviously definitive for our Lord's own understanding of His ministry, is that of the suffering servant in Isaiah 53. He would be 'despised and rejected of men, a man of sorrows, and acquainted with grief'. Above all, He would bear his people's sins:

'He was wounded for our transgressions,
   He was bruised for our iniquities;
upon Him was the chastisement that made us whole,
   and with His stripes we are healed.
All we like sheep have gone astray;
   we have turned every one to his own way;
and the Lord has laid on Him the iniquity of us all.'[17]

Christ in the Writings

The third division of the Old Testament was 'the writings', sometimes called 'the psalms' because the Psalter was the chief book of this section. Several psalms are applied to Jesus Christ in the New Testament, psalms which include references to His deity, humanity, sufferings and exaltation. Thus the words 'You are My son, today I have begotten You'[18] were used (at least in part) by God the Father in direct address to His Son at both His baptism and His transfiguration. The allusions in Psalm 8 to man as 'made a little lower than the angels' and 'crowned with glory and honour', are applied to Christ by the author of the Letter to the Hebrews. Jesus Himself quoted Ps. 22.1 from the cross 'My God, My God, why hast Thou forsaken Me?', claiming that He had personally experienced and fulfilled the terrible Godforsakenness which the psalmist expressed. He also quoted David's saying in Ps. 110.1 'The Lord says to my Lord: "Sit at My right hand, till I make Your enemies Your footstool"', and asked His critics how in their view the Messiah could be both David's Lord and David's son.

'The writings' contain, in addition, what is often called the wisdom literature of the Old Testament. The 'wise men' appear to have become a distinct group in Israel during the later period of the monarchy, alongside the prophets and the priests. They knew that the beginning of wisdom was to fear God and depart from evil. Often they extolled wisdom in glowing terms, as more precious than gold, silver and jewels, and occasionally they appeared even to personify wisdom as the agent of God's creation:

'When He established the heavens, I was there,
    when He drew a circle on the face of the deep,
when He assigned to the sea its limit, so that the waters
    might not transgress His command,
when He marked out the foundations of the earth,
then I was beside Him, like a master workman;
and I was daily His delight, rejoicing before Him
    always,
rejoicing in His inhabited world
    and delighting in the sons of men.'[19]

Christians have no difficulty in recognizing that this wisdom of God is uniquely incorporated in Jesus Christ, the personal 'Word' who was in the beginning with God and through whom all things were made.[20]

The Old Testament expectation of Christ—in the law, the prophets and the writings—is seen to have been extremely diverse. Jesus Himself summed it up in the comprehensive expression that 'the Christ should suffer . . . and enter into His glory'.[21] The apostle Peter took up the phrase, conceding that the prophets did not fully understand 'what person or time was indicated by the Spirit of Christ within them when predicting the sufferings of Christ and the subsequent glory'.[22] But this double strand of prophecy was there, representing Him as the priest who would offer Himself as a sacrifice for sin and the king whose glorious reign would know no end.

In fact, another way of summing up the Old Testament witness to Christ is to say that it depicts Him as a prophet greater than Moses, a priest greater than Aaron and a king greater than David. That is to say, He will perfectly reveal God to man, reconcile man to God and rule over man for God. In Him the Old Testament ideals of prophecy, priesthood and kingship will find their final fulfilment.

Christ in the New Testament

If the idea of discovering Christ in the Old Testament seems at first sight strange, there is no similar difficulty about finding Him in the New. The gospels tell the story from different points of view, as we shall see more fully in chapter 5, of the birth, life, death and resurrection of Jesus, and supply a sample of His words and works.

These 'memoirs of the apostles', as they used to be called in the early church, came rightly to be known as 'Gospels', for each evangelist tells his story as 'gospel' or good news of Christ and His salvation. They do not present Him as a biographer might. For they are essentially witnesses, directing their readers' attention to one they believed to be the God-man, born to save His people from their sins, whose words were words of eternal life, whose works dramatized the glory of His kingdom, who died as a ransom for sinners and rose in triumph to be Lord of all.

You might suppose that the Acts of the Apostles, which tells the story of the early days of Christianity, is more about the church than about Christ. Yet this would grievously misrepresent its nature. Luke its author is of a different persuasion. In introducing his work to Theophilus (for whom he is writing) he describes his first book (the Gospel of Luke) as containing 'all that Jesus began both to do and teach'. The implication is that the Acts story will contain all that Jesus *continued* to do and teach through His apostles. So in the Acts we listen to Christ as He was still speaking to men, though now through the great sermons of the apostles Peter and Paul which Luke records. We also see the miracles which He did through them, for 'many wonders and signs were done *through* the apostles' by Christ.[23] And we watch Christ building His own church by adding converts to it:

'And the Lord added to their number day by day those who were being saved.'[24]

The epistles extend the New Testament's witness to Christ by unfolding further the glory of His divine-human person and saving work, and by relating the life of the Christian and of the church to Him. The apostles exalt Christ as the one in whom 'all the fulness of God was pleased to dwell' and through whom we ourselves come to 'fulness of life'.[25] In Christ God has 'blessed us . . . with every spiritual blessing', they say,[26] so that we can do all things through Him who inwardly strengthens us.[27] The Christ the apostles present is an all-sufficient Christ, who is able to save to the uttermost and for all time 'those who draw near to God through Him'.[28]

The Bible's disclosure of Christ reaches its climax in the Revelation of John. He is portrayed in the vivid imagery which characterizes this book. First He appears as a glorified man 'in the midst of the lampstands'. These represent the churches, which the risen Christ is seen to patrol and superintend, so that He is able to say to each 'I know your works.'[29] Then the scene changes from earth to heaven, and Jesus Christ appears in the guise of 'a Lamb . . . , as though it had been slain'. The countless international crowd of the redeemed are even said to have 'washed their robes and made them white in the blood of the Lamb', which means that they owe their righteousness to Christ crucified alone.[30] Then towards the end of the book Christ is seen as a majestic rider on a white horse, going forth to judgment, with His name inscribed upon him 'King of kings and Lord of lords'.[31] Finally we are introduced to Him as the Heavenly Bridegroom for, we are told, 'the marriage of the Lamb has come, and his Bride has made herself ready'. His bride is the glorified Church which is then seen 'coming down out of heaven from God, prepared as a bride adorned for her husband'.[32] Almost the last words of the Revelation are 'The Spirit and the Bride say, "Come". And let him who hears say, "Come" . . . Come, Lord Jesus!'[33]

There is great diversity of content, style and purpose among the books of the Bible, and in some books the witness to Christ is indirect, even oblique. But this brief survey of the Old and New Testaments should be enough to demonstrate that 'the testimony of Jesus is the spirit of prophecy'.[34] If we want to know Christ and His salvation, it is to the Bible we must turn. For the Bible is God's own portrait of Christ. We can never know Him otherwise. As Jerome put it in the fourth century A.D., 'Ignorance of the Scriptures is ignorance of Christ'.[35]

Just as in a children's treasure hunt, one is sometimes fortunate enough to stumble immediately upon the treasure but usually has to follow laboriously from clue to clue until at last the treasure is found, so it is with Bible reading. Some verses point one direct to Christ. Others are remote clues. But a painstaking pursuit of the clues will ultimately lead every reader to that treasure whose worth is beyond price.

Through Faith

The Scriptures are able to instruct us for salvation, the apostle Paul wrote, 'through faith in Christ Jesus'. Since their purpose (or the purpose of the divine author through them) is to bring us to salvation, and since salvation is in Christ, they point us to Christ, as we have seen. But their object in pointing us to Christ is not simply that we should know about Him and understand Him, nor even that we should admire Him, but that we should put our trust in Him. Scripture bears witness to Christ not in order to satisfy our curiosity but in order to elicit our faith.

There is much misunderstanding about faith. It is commonly supposed to be a leap in the dark, totally incompatible with reason. This is not so. True faith is never unreasonable, because its object is always trust-worthy. When we human beings trust one another, the reasonableness of our trust depends on the relative trustworthiness of the people concerned. But the Bible bears witness to Jesus Christ as absolutely trustworthy. It tells us who He is and what He has done, and the evidence it supplies for His unique person and work is extremely compelling. As we expose ourselves to the biblical witness to this Christ and as we feel its impact—profound yet simple, varied yet unanimous—God creates faith within us. We receive the testimony. We believe.

This is what Paul meant when he wrote:

'So faith comes from what is heard, and what is heard comes by the preaching of Christ'.[36]

We have seen that God's purpose in and through the Bible is severely practical. He has ordained it as His chief instrument for bringing men to 'salvation', understood in its widest and fullest sense. The whole Bible is a gospel of salvation, and the gospel is 'the power of God for salvation to every one who has faith'.[37] So it points its many fingers unerringly to Christ, so that its readers will see Him, believe in Him and be saved.

The apostle John writes something very similar at the end of his Gospel. He has recorded only a selection of the signs of Jesus, he says, for Jesus performed many others. He goes on:

'But these are written that you may believe that Jesus is the Christ, the Son of God, and that believing you may have life in His name'.[38]

John sees the ultimate purpose of Scripture ('what is written') just as Paul sees it. John calls it 'life', Paul 'salvation', but the words are virtually synonymous. Both apostles are further agreed that this life or salvation is in Christ, and that to receive it we must believe in Him. The sequence, Scripture—Christ—faith—salvation, is exactly the same. Scripture testifies to Christ in order to evoke faith in Christ, in order to bring life to the believer.

The conclusion is simple. Whenever we read the Bible, we must look for Christ. And we must go on looking until we see and so believe. Only as we continue to appropriate by faith the riches of Christ which are disclosed to us in Scripture shall we grow into spiritual maturity, and become men and women of God who are 'complete, equipped for every good work'.

For Further Reading

The Unfolding Message of the Bible (The Harmony and Unity of the Scriptures) by Campbell Morgan (Pickering and Inglis 1961, 416 pages). A simple, informal, readable introduction to the Bible's sixty-six books, one chapter to each book or group. The Old Testament is presented in terms of 'The Need' and the New Testament in terms of 'The Supply'. Christ is shown as the heart of the Scriptures – prophet, priest and king foreshadowed throughout the Old Testament.

Meet the Book by George E. Harpur (Pickering and Inglis 1962, 128 pages). A basic introduction, containing both information and wisdom. The book is divided into four sections entitled 'Meet it' (the form and history of the Bible), 'Trust it' (chapters on inspiration, authority and reliability), 'Know it' (contents and interpretation) and 'Use it' (its study, ministry and effects).

NOTES

1 2 Tim. 3.15–17
2 Luke 1.68–75
3 Rom. 8.24
4 Rom. 8.21; 1 Cor. 15.28
5 Heb. 2.3
6 John 5.39
7 Lk. 24.27
8 Lk. 24.44
9 Mk. 1.15
10 Mt. 13.16, 17
11 Gen. 3.15; 12.3; 49.10
12 Deut. 18.15, 18b
13 1 Pet. 1.3, 4
14 Gal. 3.23, 24
15 2 Sam. 7.8–17
16 Is. 9.6, 7
17 Is. 53.5, 6
18 Ps. 2.7
19 Prov. 8.27–31
20 see Jn. 1.1–3; Col. 2.3
21 Lk. 24.26
22 1 Pet. 1.11

23 Acts 2.43
24 Acts 2.47
25 Col. 1.19; 2.9, 10
26 Eph. 1.3
27 Phil. 4.13
28 Heb. 7.25
29 Rev. 1–3
30 Rev. 5.6; 7.14
31 Rev. 19.11–16
32 see Rev. 19.7–9; 21.2
33 Rev. 22.17, 20
34 Rev. 19.10
35 In the prologue to his commentary on Isaiah, quoted in Vatican II's *Dogmatic Constitution on Divine Revelation*, para. 25
36 Rom. 10.17
37 Rom. 1.16
38 Jn. 20.31

2. THE LAND OF THE BIBLE

God's purpose to call out from the world a people for Himself began to unfold in a particular part of the world's surface and during a particular period of the world's history. It is not possible to understand its meaning, therefore, without some knowledge of its historical and geographical setting.

Yet the very mention of history and geography, especially Bible history and Bible geography, is enough to switch some people off. They shudder as they recall boring RE lessons at school, with date-lists of dreary Israelite kings to memorize and Paul's interminable missionary journeys to plot on a map. If you feel like that, I sympathize with you. I suffered that way too. So evidently did the theological student who was required in an exam to distinguish between the prophets Elijah and Elisha. As he did not have the foggiest notion which was which, it is rumoured that his essay began: 'Let us not haggle over the differences between these two truly great

31

The Fertile Crescent

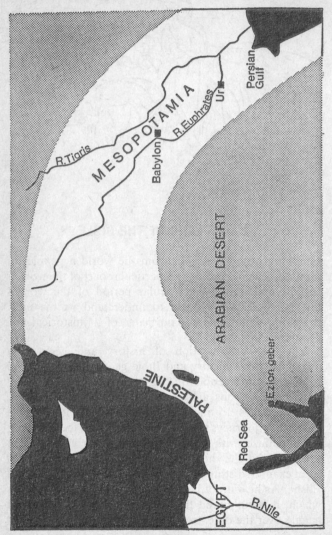

men. But let us rather give a list of the kings of Israel and Judah in their chronological order.'

Some folk who have no taste for either history or geography may ask rather impatiently why God did not give us instead a simple set of dogmas to believe and rules to obey. Why did He have to reveal Himself in a rather remote historical and geographical context, so that we have to struggle to understand the context before we can grasp the revelation? One reply might be: 'Because God chose to do it that way' and 'Stop asking impertinent questions.' But the questions are perfectly proper ones.

A better answer would be that the living God is a personal God, who made us as persons in His own image and insists on treating as persons the persons He has made. So the whole process of revelation has been the self-disclosure of a Person to persons, to real persons like ourselves who actually lived in a certain place at a certain time. In saying this, I am not denying that God has revealed His truth in words. I am rather asserting that His revelation has been 'personal' and 'propositional' at one and the same time. That is, the truths He has revealed have not descended from heaven by parachute. They have not appeared in disjointed form as 'The Thoughts of God', comparable to Chairman Mao's. They have rather been made known in and through the living experience of human beings, culminating in His own Son, the Word made flesh.

Moreover, if God had simply supplied us with a systematic catalogue of dos and don'ts for everyday belief and behaviour, it would have been far too abstract to be useful. And if it had been expressed in the idiom of one age or generation, it would have been largely meaningless to others. But as it is, God revealed Himself in personal situations, which being human are concrete and readily intelligible in every generation. Their record in Scripture enables us to 'see' for ourselves.

God's dealings with the nation of Israel and with individuals are recorded, we are told, 'for our instruction'.[1] And the instruction they give consists of both encouragement and warning.

'The encouragement of the Scriptures'[2] is tremendous. Even the great men of the Biblical story, it is emphasized, were 'of like nature' with us.[3] Yet we watch them overcoming in their struggle with temptation and doubt; refusing to bow down to idols and willing to accept death rather than compromise their allegiance to the living God; believing the promises of God in spite of every evidence to the contrary; standing alone in an age of prevailing apostasy; loving and serving their own generation; and bravely bearing witness to the truth.

Scripture contains warning as well as encouragement, for it refuses to conceal the faults even of its great men. It tells us frankly how righteous Noah got drunk; how once Abraham, the giant of faith, fell so deeply into unbelief that he was ready even to expose his wife to moral danger in order to save his own skin; how Jacob schemed and Joseph boasted; how Moses, the meekest man on earth, lost his temper; how David, who found favour in the sight of God, yet committed theft, murder and adultery in a single surrender to passion; how Job, 'blameless and upright, one who feared God and turned away from evil', yet, under the provocation of great adversity, cried out in bitterness and cursed the day of his birth; and how the whole nation of Israel, despite its many unique privileges, broke the covenant of God. The Bible is equally candid with its New Testament characters. They too were men of flesh and blood like us, who gave way sometimes to unbelief, compromise, boastfulness, indiscipline and disobedience. 'Now these things are warnings to us'[4]

God wants to deal with us in our situation of time and place, as He dealt with the Biblical characters in theirs.

So to understand His ways with us, we must understand His ways with them. And to understand this, we must know something of both where and when it all happened. We must be able to visualize it. So our look at the land of the Bible in this chapter and at the story of the Bible in the next two becomes a fascinating, even indispensable study. For this history and this geography constitute the arena in which God chose uniquely to speak and to act.

It used to be seriously argued by Christian geographers in the middle ages that Jerusalem was the centre of the earth. Their maps illustrated their belief. And in the ancient Church of the Holy Sepulchre in Jerusalem (which is built over the supposed site of the crucifixion and resurrection of Jesus) a stone is let into the floor to mark what was thought to be the precise spot.

Of course this is sheer nonsense, geographically speaking. Theologically, however, Christians would defend it as true. To them Palestine is 'the Holy Land', a region distinct from all others. It is also the centre of the world's history and geography in this sense that here lay 'the promised land' which God pledged to Abraham some two thousand years before Christ; here the Saviour of the world both lived and died; and here the Christian mission was born, which was to outlive the Roman empire and change the course of world history.

Further, Christians believe in the providence of God. We cannot therefore imagine that the choice of Palestine as the stage for the drama of salvation was an accident. One of its obvious features is that it acts as a kind of bridge between three continents. Europe, Asia and Africa converge at the eastern seaboard of the Mediterranean, and their citizens have ever mingled with each other on its trade routes by sea and land. Consequently, not only has Palestine been invaded and subjugated by armies from all three—first Egyptian, then Assyrian, Babylonian

35

and Persian, and finally Greek and Roman—but it became an admirable springboard for spiritual counter-attack, the soldiers of Jesus Christ marching north, south, east and west to the conquest of the world. 'You shall be My witnesses,' His last words to them had been, 'in Jerusalem and in all Judea and Samaria and to the end of the earth'.[5] Strategically, therefore, God had set Jerusalem 'in the centre of the nations'.[6] If Christ's witnesses had taught more clearly the middle eastern origins of Christianity, one wonders if the gospel would ever have become so closely associated in the minds of Africans and Asians with the white and the western world.

'Palestine'—the word came originally from the Philistines who occupied a small south western section of it—is itself only a part of the arena of Old Testament history. The wider scene has often been called the 'Fertile Crescent', because it sweeps round in a semi-circle from Egypt to Mesopotamia, from the Nile valley to the alluvial plain watered by the Euphrates and Tigris rivers, enclosing the arid Arabian desert. In order to understand the history of God's people, one needs to keep this crescent in mind, and not least the two great rivers which form its extremities. For God called Abraham from Ur of the Chaldees, situated only nine miles from the River Euphrates in Southern Iraq, and Moses from Egypt where he had narrowly escaped drowning as a baby in the River Nile. The very words 'Egypt' and 'Babylonia' reminded Israelites of the saving initiatives of their God, for these countries were the scenes of their two bitter captivities, from which their God had delivered them.

Palestine

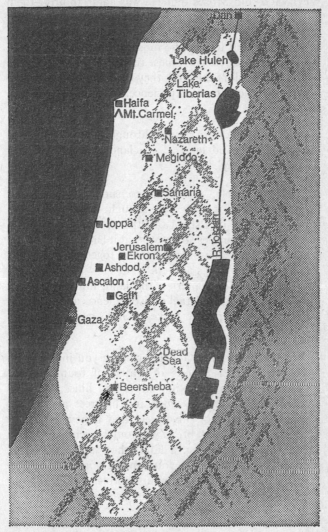

A Good Land

When God told Moses that He was about to bring them out of Egypt into Canaan, He described it as 'a good and broad land, a land flowing with milk and honey',[7] adding later that it was 'the most glorious of all lands'.[8] And when the twelve spies reported, whom Moses had sent to explore the land, they confirmed this description from their own experience. Joshua and Caleb said:

'The land, which we passed through to spy it out, is an exceedingly good land . . ., a land which flows with milk and honey'.[9]

They were able, moreover, to supply evidence for their assertion, for they had brought back with them from the Valley of Eshcol (a little north of Hebron) a single cluster of grapes so heavy that it had to be slung on a pole and carried by two of them, together with some pomegranates and figs as well.[10]

Then, just before entering the land, after a delay of forty years owing to Israel's disobedience and unbelief, Moses urged the people to keep God's commandments and added:

'For the Lord your God is bringing you into a good land, a land of brooks of water, of fountains and springs, flowing forth in valleys and hills, a land of wheat and barley, of vines and fig trees and pomegranates, a land of olive trees and honey, a land in which you will eat bread without scarcity, in which you will lack nothing, a land whose stones are iron, and out of whose hills you can dig copper. And you shall eat and be full, and you shall bless the Lord your God for the good land He has given you'.[11]

Although Palestinian farmers have to work hard to

secure a good yield, this is still an accurate description of the country's fertility and produce.

The country we are describing extends only about 200 miles from north to south and 100 miles from west to east. It is hemmed in by natural boundaries. To the north rises the mountainous mass of the Lebanon (meaning 'white' because of its snows) and the Anti-lebanon, the valley between being known as 'the entrance of Hamath'. To the west lies the Mediterranean or 'the Great Sea', and to the east and south the forbidding deserts of Arabia and of Zin.[12]

Several popular expressions were used to refer to the whole country from north to south. One was 'from the entrance of Hamath as far as the Sea of the Arabah', that is the Dead Sea.[13] But the commonest was simply 'from Dan to Beersheba',[14] Dan being Israel's most northerly city, while Beersheba was its most southerly, situated at the edge of the desert of Zin, about halfway between the Mediterranean and the southern tip of the Dead Sea.[15]

Visitors to the Holy Land, provided they have an opportunity to explore it adequately, are struck by the great variety of its terrain. The contrast is nowhere greater than between the 'seas' or 'lakes' at the northern and southern ends of the Jordan River. For the colourful beauty of Galilee—with its blue, mountain-girt lake, its carpet of springtime flowers and its distant backdrop of snow-capped Mount Hermon to the north—is a veritable paradise in comparison with the heat, the stench and the desolation of the Dead Sea and its environs.

The Biblical record often alludes to the different 'regions' into which Palestine is divided. For example, its inhabitants are described as living 'in the Arabah, in the hill country and in the lowland, and in the Negeb, and by the seacoast'.[16] The 'Arabah' is the deep gorge of the Jordan Valley running south to the Gulf of Aqabah.

The 'hillcountry' refers to the mountains of Judea, while the 'lowland' is the Shephelah, its western foothills. The 'Negeb', meaning 'the dry', is the great southern desert whose other name is the wilderness of Zin, and the 'seacoast' lies along the Mediterranean.

Perhaps a simpler way to remember the map of Palestine is to visualize four strips of country running parallel from north to south. The most striking is the Jordan valley. The river cuts its way deep between two mountain ranges—the central highlands which form the backbone of Palestine (its western slopes going down to the coastal plain) and the eastern tableland beyond which lies the desert. So the four strips between the sea and the desert are the coastland, the central highlands, the Jordan valley and the eastern tableland. We shall look at each in turn.

The Coastal Strip

The coastal strip varies in breadth from a few hundred yards where Mount Carmel juts out into the sea (and the modern port of Haifa is situated) to some thirty miles at the southern end. This southern part was the ancient land of the Philistines. It is here that the five main Philistine cities were located—Gaza the most southerly, on the great coastal road which runs up from Egypt about three miles inland, Ascalon twelve miles north and on the sea, Ashdod eight miles farther north and on the road again, with Ekron farther north and more inland, and Gath in the middle of the plain.

The Shephelah or lowland lies immediately east of the Plain of Philistia. It is not surprising to read, therefore, that 'the Philistines . . . made raids on the cities in the Shephelah'.[17] Its sycamore trees were proverbial; so it could be said that Solomon 'made cedar as plentiful as the sycamore of the Shephelah'.[18] Its slopes are, in fact,

Palestine/Coastal Strip

Central Highlands

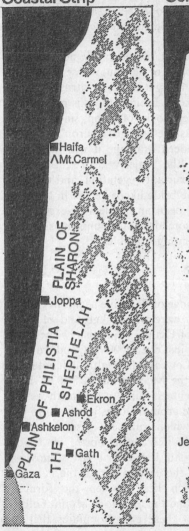

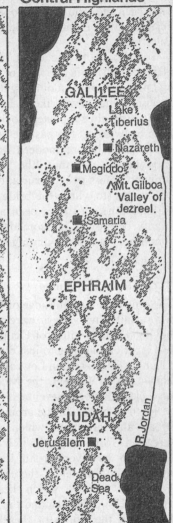

the foothills of the central plateau. They rise steadily from about 500 feet at Gath to 1,300 feet ten miles to the east. Then the mountains proper begin, and a further ten miles east lies Hebron, at 3,300 feet the highest city in Palestine.

Going back to the coast, immediately north of the plain of Philistia is the plain of Sharon, whose main town and port is Joppa. In our day it is rich in citrus orchards. Precisely what it was like in Biblical times is not certain, but it certainly supported flocks of sheep, since we read once or twice of 'the pasture lands of Sharon'.[19] On the other hand, before modern drainage it will have been very marshy, so that 'the majesty of . . . Sharon'[20] probably refers to its luxuriant vegetation, and the 'rose of Sharon' (to whom the bride likens herself in the Song of Solomon) may have been an emblem of exceptional beauty because it blossomed in such unpromising surroundings, like 'a lily among brambles'.[21]

The Central Highlands

The central mountain range of Palestine begins in Galilee, whose hills and valleys were the background of Jesus' boyhood and of much of His public ministry. The peaks of Upper Galilee rise to just over 3000 feet, and from the hills above Nazareth in Lower Galilee, although not much higher than 1500 feet, the Mediterranean Sea is visible on a clear day only seventeen miles to the north-west.

South of Nazareth the ground slopes gently down to a broad alluvial plain, which runs in a south-easterly direction from the Mediterranean north of Mount Carmel to the River Jordan. Its western part is known as the Plain of Esdraelon; the eastern part is the narrower Valley of Jezreel, which lies between the formerly volcanic Hill of Moreh and the limestone Mount Gilboa. It was on the slopes of these two mountains that the

Philistines and the Israelites encamped, facing each other across the valley, before the final battle in which King Saul died:

> 'Now the Philistines fought against Israel; and the men of Israel fled before the Philistines, and fell slain on Mount Gilboa ... And David lamented with this lamentation over Saul and Jonathan his son ... "Thy glory, O Israel, is slain upon thy high places! How are the mighty fallen! ... Ye mountains of Gilboa, let there be no dew or rain upon you, nor upsurging of the deep! For there the shield of the mighty was defiled, the shield of Saul, not anointed with oil".'[22]

At the southern edge of the middle of the plain of Esdraelon, on a prominent site at the foot of the Carmel range, lies the fortress town of Megiddo. For centuries it has guarded the entrance to the main pass through the mountains to the south. It was one of the cities which King Solomon rebuilt and fortified to accommodate his horses and chariots[23]. Here also two kings of Judah died, Ahaziah who was shot by Jehu,[24] and Josiah who was killed while attempting to stop Pharaoh Neco of Egypt from going to the help of the Assyrians.[25]

South of the plain of Esdraelon lies the hill country of Manasseh and Ephraim, well covered with vineyards on their west-facing slopes, and still farther south the hill country of Judah. These two mountainous regions were the focal point of Israel's history during the period of the divided monarchy. For the capital of the northern kingdom was Samaria (in the land of Manesseh-Ephraim) and the capital of the southern kingdom was Jerusalem (in the land of Judah).

Jerusalem is built on a mountain surrounded by mountains. God's 'holy mountain, beautiful in elevation', the psalmist could sing, 'is the joy of all the earth.' Again, 'as the mountains are round about Jerusalem, so the Lord is round about His people'.[26] The Mount of Olives lies immediately to the east of Jerusalem, across the Kidron valley, and from this summit the road runs east through the most barren land imaginable, dropping more than 3000 feet to Jericho and on to the Dead Sea. It was while making this two-day journey on foot that the traveller in Christ's parable was attacked by brigands and rescued by the Good Samaritan.

The whole area between Jerusalem and the Dead Sea is known as the Wilderness of Judea, and it was somewhere in this scene of desolation that Jesus spent forty days following His baptism, fasting and being tempted by the devil.

The Jordan Valley

The Jordan Valley is part of the Great Rift Valley which stretches for 4,000 miles from Asia Minor through the Red Sea to the Rift Valley lakes of East Africa. But the River Jordan itself is only about eighty miles in total length, excluding its meanderings. It rises in Mount Hermon, a 9,000 feet shoulder of the Antilebanon mass, and then maintains a steady descent ('Jordan' means 'descender') through Lake Huleh and Lake Tiberias until it peters out in the Dead Sea. At Huleh it is still above sea level (about 230 feet), but Lake Tiberias is nearly 700 feet below, while its final descent takes it to about 1,300 feet below at the Dead Sea, whose bottom at over 2,500 feet is the deepest point on the surface of the earth.

Lake Huleh is known in the Bible as 'the waters of Merom' but does not feature prominently in the Biblical narrative.[27] It has always been the haunt rather of birds than of men—Purple Herons still nest in its tall papyrus reeds—although recently most of it was drained for agricultural land.

Lake Tiberias is called in the Gospels sometimes 'the

Palestine/Jordan Valley

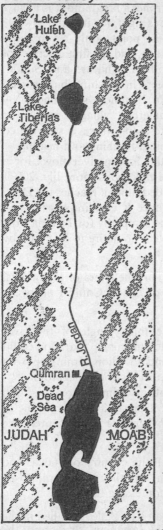

Lake Huleh

Lake Tiberias

R. Jordan

Qumran

Dead Sea

JUDAH

MOAB

Eastern Tableland

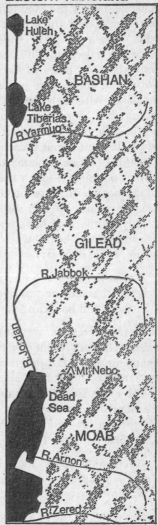

Lake Huleh

BASHAN

Lake Tiberias

R. Yarmuq

GILEAD

R. Jabbok

R. Jordan

Mt. Nebo

Dead Sea

MOAB

R. Arnon

R. Zered

Sea of Chinnereth' (or Gennesaret) but usually 'the Sea of Galilee', although to Luke the much-travelled evangelist who knew the Mediterranean first-hand it is always merely a 'lake'[28]. Indeed, he is right, for it is only twelve miles long and—at its widest point—only seven miles across. It is deep and full of fish, and the first disciples of Jesus, the two pairs of brothers, Andrew and Simon, James and John, were partners in a fishing business on the lake. Although the lake is almost surrounded by mountains, there were numerous villages round its northern and western shores, and these Jesus visited when He went about preaching, teaching and healing.

South of Lake Tiberias the Jordan river flows for a further 65 miles (though the mileage is more like 200 if all the meanderings are included) until it reaches the Dead Sea. For much of this distance it is unimpressive and muddy, so that one has some sympathy for Naaman the leprous Syrian general who had no desire to be cured by having to wash in it:

'Are not Abana and Pharpar, the rivers of Damascus, better than all the waters of Israel? Could I not wash in them and be clean?'[29]

More impressive was the thick jungle of the river valley, a famous haunt of wild animals, so that God could liken Himself in His judgments to 'a lion coming up from the jungle of the Jordan against a strong sheepfold'.[30]

The exact site of the baptisms administered by John the Baptist is unknown, but it must have been at one of the fords a few miles from where the Jordan enters the Dead Sea. Thus:

'There went out to him all the country of Judea, and all the people of Jerusalem; and they were baptized by him in the river Jordan, confessing their sins'.[31]

The whole of the Palestinian Rift Valley is called in the Old Testament 'the Arabah', meaning 'dry', and the

Dead Sea is 'the Sea of the Arabah' or 'the Salt Sea'· This is forty-eight miles long and a scene of almost unrelieved desolation. Its eastern shore is overlooked by the sheer cliffs of the mountains of Moab, while on the west are the barren slopes of the mountains of Judah. Here (at Qumran) lived the Essene monastic community before and during the time of Christ, and here in our time the Dead Sea Scrolls were found in some of the caves which honeycomb the hills.

The heat is so intense (up to 110° in the summer), the evaporation so great and the rainfall so small, that the water level of the Dead Sea remains constant despite the inflowing streams and the absence of all outflow. As a result, the chemical deposits in the water (especially salt, potash and magnesium) are highly concentrated, and no fish can survive.[32] It seems likely that Sodom and Gomorrah, 'the cities of the plain', were situated in the area now covered by the southern tip of the Dead Sea. And it is not impossible that the 'brimstone and fire' which the Lord 'rained' on them, together with the 'pillar of salt' into which Lot's wife was changed, were the results of an earthquake and eruption which God used to destroy them for their wickedness.[33]

The Arabah continues south of the Dead Sea until it reaches the Red Sea at the Gulf of Aqabah. Here was the port of Ezion Geber (the equivalent of the modern Elath), giving Israel access by sea to the trade of Africa and Asia. For 'King Solomon built a fleet of ships at Ezion-Geber . . .'.[34] Copper was exported from the nearby mines which Solomon developed, while imports included such exotic items as 'gold, silver, ivory, apes and peacocks'.[35]

The Eastern Tableland

The fourth strip of Palestinian country we have to consider is the eastern tableland, between the Jordan Valley and the Arabian desert. This was the area inherited by two and a half of Israel's twelve tribes:

> 'Gad and Reuben and half the tribe of Manasseh . . . received their inheritance beyond the Jordan eastward'.[36]

It is a vast plateau stretching for about 250 miles from north to south, divided by four rivers which have cut deep canyons on their way westwards into the River Jordan or the Dead Sea. The first is the River Yarmuq, which flows into the Jordan just south of Lake Tiberias. The second is the River Jabbok which reaches the Jordan approximately half way between Lake Tiberias and the Dead Sea. It was here that 'Jacob was left alone, and a man wrestled with him until the breaking of the day'.[37] The River Arnon flows into the middle of the Dead Sea and the River Zered into its southern tip. These rivers formed natural frontiers for Israel's neighbouring tribes, Ammon claiming the territory between the Jabbok and the Arnon, Moab that between the Arnon and the Zered (though often spilling over to the north), and Edom that south of the Zered.

Perhaps it is easiest, however, to visualize the plateau east of the Jordan by remembering the main divisions which Denis Baly describes in his *The Geography of the Bible*.[38] Bashan, the tableland east of Lake Tiberias, he calls 'the land of the farmer', for though it was probably well wooded in Bible times it was famed for its corn crop and for its rams, lambs, goats and bulls, 'all of them fatlings of Bashan'.[39]

South of Bashan was Gilead, a term covering virtually the whole of Transjordan between Lake Tiberias and the Dead Sea. This is 'the land of the highlander'. As the terrain rises to over 3,000 feet, the rainfall is considerable and brings fertility to both forest and vineyard. The grapes of Gilead were unrivalled throughout Palestine and 'the balm of Gilead' (an aromatic spice of some kind) was famous. The caravan of Ishmaelites to whom Joseph was sold by his brothers were 'coming from Gilead, with their camels bearing gum, balm and myrrh, on their way to carry it down to Egypt'.[40]

Continuing our journey south in Transjordan, Moab comes next, occupying the mountainous territory east of the Dead Sea. Apart from the deep gorges of the river Arnon and of some smaller streams, most of Moab is a high plateau. Denis Baly calls it 'the land of the shepherd':

'Everywhere . . . there are sheep, great flocks and converging lines of them, like the spokes of a limitless wheel, moving in clouds of golden dust to be given their water at the well'.[41]

So too we read in the Bible:

'Now Mesha King of Moab was a sheep breeder; and he had to deliver annually to the King of Israel a hundred thousand lambs, and the wool of a hundred thousand rams'.[42]

It was from the mountains of Moab (Mt. Nebo, to be precise) that Moses viewed the promised land before he died, and on the plains of Moab that the children of Israel encamped before crossing the Jordan to take possession of it.[43]

The most southerly section of Transjordan is Edom. At its highest points it rises to about 3,500 feet, towering above the deserts to the west, east and south. Denis Baly names it 'the land of the trader', for through it passed the great eastern trade route known as 'the King's Highway'. It was because of Edom's refusal to allow Israel to use this route on their way to the promised land that there was long-standing enmity between the two countries.[44]

Such is the 'good land' which the Lord their God gave to Israel. It was a country for farmers, who kept livestock and cultivated the arable land.

Their livestock consisted mostly of sheep and goats, which roamed in huge mixed flocks over the hills and the steppe. The goats supplied milk and the black hair of which Bedouin tents were made, while the sheep gave milk, meat and wool. Because Palestinian shepherds kept their sheep more for wool than for mutton, however, quite an intimate relationship grew up between them over the years. The shepherd would lead his sheep, not drive them. He would know them individually, and call them by name, while they for their part would know his voice and follow him. It seemed only natural that God should reveal Himself as the 'Shepherd of Israel' who would 'gather the lambs in His arms, ... carry them in His bosom, and gently lead those that are with young',[45] and indeed that the godly Israelite should be able to affirm:

'The Lord is my shepherd, I shall not want; He makes me lie down in green pastures. He leads me beside still waters'.[46]

The Lord Jesus developed the metaphor further, calling Himself 'the Good Shepherd' and affirming that He would both lay down His life for the sheep and go out into the desert in search of only one that was lost.[47]

Though many Israelite farmers kept livestock, even more cultivated the soil. The three main products of Palestine are bracketed together in many Biblical passages. Before they entered the land, this was the reward which they were promised for their obedience:

'The Lord your God ... will ... bless ... the fruit of your ground, your grain and your wine and your oil.'

When they had taken possession of it, they proved God's faithfulness in giving 'wine to gladden the heart of man, oil to make his face shine, and bread to strengthen man's heart'. But when they rebelled against Him He witheld these blessings—through famine or pestilence or locusts—until they repented and He could say to them:

'Behold, I am sending to you grain, wine and oil, and you will be satisfied'.[48]

The grain from which their bread came was mostly wheat and barley, while the wine came from the extensive vineyards, and the oil (principally for cooking) from the olive-yards. Olive trees are particularly hardy, being able to survive in shallow soil and to withstand long periods of drought.

Other fruits of ancient Israel were pomegranates, and especially figs, so that the sweetest Israelite dream of peace and security in the Messianic kingdom was:

'they shall sit every man under his vine and under his fig tree, and none shall make them afraid'.[49]

For a good harvest the land was entirely dependent upon rain. The Israelite knew that there was no greater blessing of God. It was 'the living God who made the heaven and the earth and the sea and all that is in them' who gave 'from heaven rains and fruitful seasons', thus bearing witness to His own faithfulness. And so great is His grace to all mankind, Jesus emphasized, that 'He makes His sun rise on the evil and on the good, and sends rain on the just and on the unjust'.[50]

Generally speaking, the Palestinian rainy seasons are predictable. The summer extends from May/June to September/October, and during these five months rain is virtually unknown, so that Samuel's prayer for rain during wheat harvest was a request for a miracle. Indeed, 'snow in summer or rain in harvest' is as out of place as 'honour . . . for a fool'.[51] During this dry season there is only the dew to bring moisture, and the morning mist. But both dissipate speedily when the sun rises, and their disappearance is used as a picture of idolatrous Israel when the judgment of God falls:

> 'They shall be like the morning mist or like the dew that goes early away'.[52]

From about mid-October, however, the rain clouds begin to form, and when the rain finally comes, often accompanied by thunder, there is nothing to do but run for shelter. Denis Baly describes the scene:

> 'Jesus quoted it as a well-known occurrence that a badly built house might collapse during the rainy season (Mt. 7.27) and, indeed, it is only when one has seen a storm sweeping in from the Mediterranean across the Palestinian hills or the torrents pouring down the precipitous slopes into the lake of Galilee that one knows quite what a concentrated fury is contained in those words, "and the rain fell, and the floods came, and the winds blew and beat against that house".'[53]

The beginning of the rainy season was usually termed 'the early rains', and, far from being regarded as destructive, they were looked upon as beneficial, indeed indispensable. Without them ploughing was impossible, for the sun-baked earth was hard as iron.[54] But once the rains had started and begun to soften the soil, especially if their arrival was late, the farmer must brave the weather and get on with his ploughing if he was to be able to sow his fields in time for harvest. Jesus used this as a picture of Christian courage and perseverance:

> 'No one who puts his hand to the plough and looks back is fit for the kingdom of God'.[55]

If the 'early rains' at the start of the rainy season (from November) were essential to ploughing, the 'latter rains' at its end (in March and April) were essential to reaping. Without them the corn would remain thin and desiccated; it was the rain which swelled and matured the grain for the harvest. And when the fields were finally 'white for harvest', the labourers would put in their sickles.[56] The corn would then be tied into sheaves and carted by donkeys or camels to the threshing floor, a flat hardened surface at the top of a local hillock. There it would be first threshed by animal hooves or a sledge[57] and afterwards winnowed. Tossed into the air with a pitch fork, the precious golden grain would fall to the earth to be garnered, while the wind would blow the chaff away. This separation of wheat from chaff became a common image for the divine judgment.[58]

So 'the early and the latter rain', sometimes called 'the autumn rain and the spring rain',[59] were a necessary prelude to a good harvest. God had Himself linked the rain and the harvest together and promised them to His obedient people:

'If you will obey My commandments which I command you this day, to love the Lord your God, and to serve Him with all your heart and with all your soul, He will give the rain for your land in its season, the early rain and the later rain, that you may gather in your grain and your wine and your oil'.[60]

Wise farmers knew this and waited for 'the precious fruit' of the earth, being patient over it until it receives the early and the late rain'.[61] Consequently, when the rains were given they were full of thanksgiving to God for His mercy. No more poetic account of His harvest blessings occurs in Scripture than in Psalm 65. Notice the reference both to the early rains which water the hard ground, 'settling its ridges, softening it with showers', and to the 'crown' of the year some eight months later when 'the valleys deck themselves with grain':

'Thou visitest the earth and waterest it, Thou greatly enrichest it; the river of God is full of water; thou providest their grain, for so Thou hast prepared it. Thou waterest its furrows abundantly, settling its ridges, softening it with showers, and blessing its growth. Thou crownest the year with Thy bounty; the tracks of Thy chariot drip with fatness. The pastures of the wilderness drip, the hills gird themselves with joy, the meadows clothe themselves with flocks, the valleys deck themselves with grain, they shout and sing together for joy.'[62]

The Three Annual Festivals

In the light of Israel's closeness to the soil as a farming community, it is not surprising that their three annual festivals had an agricultural as well as a religious significance. In them they worshipped the God of nature and the God of grace as the one God, Lord of the earth and of Israel.

The Feast of the Passover, followed immediately by the Feast of Unleavened Bread, commemorated primarily Israel's redemption from Egypt. But it also took place about the middle of April when the first sheaf of ripe barley could be waved humbly and gratefully before the Lord.

The second was the Feast of the Firstfruits or Harvest, also called the Feast of Weeks or Pentecost because it was celebrated seven weeks or fifty days after the Passover, that is, at about the beginning of June. It was a thanksgiving for the completed grain harvest—wheat as well as barley. Later it came to be regarded also as commemorating the giving of the law at Mt. Sinai, perhaps because in connection with it Israel was told:

'You shall remember that you were a slave in Egypt;

and you shall be careful to observe these statutes'.[63]

The last of the three annual festivals was the Feast of Booths or Tabernacles. For seven days the people had to dwell in booths made out of tree branches. God's purpose in requiring this was clear:

'that your generation may know that I made the people of Israel dwell in booths when I brought them out of the land of Egypt'.[64]

But this festival was also known as the Feast of Ingathering, for it took place in mid-October, six months later than the Passover, by which time each year the produce of vineyard and oliveyard as well as grainfield had been gathered in.

The observance of these three annual festivals was obligatory. God had said:

'Three times in the year you shall keep a feast to Me. You shall keep the feast of unleavened bread . . . You shall keep the feast of harvest, of the first fruits of your labour, of what you sow in the field. You shall keep the feast of ingathering at the end of the year, when you gather in from the field the fruit of your labour'.[65]

From one point of view these festivals commemorated the signal mercies of the covenant God of Israel who first redeemed His people from their Egyptian bondage, then gave them the law at Sinai and then provided for them during their wanderings in the wilderness. From another point of view the three feasts were all harvest festivals, marking respectively the beginning of the barley harvest, the end of the grain harvest, and the end of the fruit harvest.

So Israel was taught to honour Jehovah both as God of creation and as God of salvation. The two themes were brought together in what the people of Israel were to do when they had come into the land of promise:

'You shall take some of the first of all the fruit of the ground, . . . put it in a basket, . . . go to the priest . . . and say to him, "I declare this day to the Lord your God that I have come into the land which the Lord swore to our fathers to give us. . . . And behold, now I bring the first of the fruit of the ground, which Thou, O Lord, hast given me" . . . and you shall rejoice in all the good which the Lord your God has given to you . . . .'[66]

Here was rich symbolism indeed. The basket of fruit was a token of 'all the good' which God had given Israel. It was the fruit of the ground, fruit which God had caused to grow. But from what ground? From ground which God had also given them, as He had sworn to their fathers. The fruit was a sacrament of both creation and redemption, for it was the fruit of the promised land.

For Further Reading

The Geography of the Bible by Denis Baly (Lutterworth 1957, 303 pages). A descriptive survey of the whole of Palestine, both general and regional, by one who lived in the country for 15 years. Well illustrated by the author's own maps, charts and black-and-white photographs.

Holy Fields (The Background of Bible Lands and Places) by J. Howard Kitchen (Paternoster 1955, 160 pages). After an introductory chapter on the nations of the Fertile Crescent, the country is described region by region. The last two chapters are on Jerusalem city and the subsequent history of Palestine. There are ten maps. The author was an Australian missionary who lectured in Old Testament at Chungking Theological Seminary, West China, before the Communist occupation in 1949.

The Way It Was in Bible Times by Merrill T. Gilbertson (Augsburg 1959, Lutterworth 1961, 142 pages). A short, simple book by a Lutheran pastor on the cultural background of the Bible. There are chapters on Israelite homes, food and clothing, social and religious customs, occupations, measurements and education, illustrated by black-and-white drawings.

NOTES

1 Rom. 15.4; 1 Cor. 10.11
2 Rom. 15.4
3 This expression is used with regard both to an Old Testament prophet like Elijah and to a New Testament apostle like Paul. See Jas. 5.17 and Acts 14.15
4 1 Cor. 10.6, 11
5 Acts 1.8
6 Ezek. 5.5
7 Ex. 3.8
8 Ezek. 20.6, 15
9 Num. 14.6–8
10 Num. 13.23, 24
11 Deut. 8.7–10
12 These boundaries are described in Num. 34.1–15
13 e.g. 2 Kings 14.25
14 e.g. Judges 20.1; 1 Sam. 3.20; 2 Sam. 3.10; 1 Kings 4.25
15 It was to Beersheba that the prophet Elijah fled when his life was threatened by Queen Jezebel. See 1 Kings 19.1–3
16 Deut. 1.7
17 2 Chron. 28.18
18 1 Kings 10.27

19 1 Chron. 5.16 cf. 27.29
20 Is. 35.2
21 Song of Solomon 2.1, 2
22 1 Sam. 31.1; 2 Sam. 1.17, 19, 21
23 1 Kings 9.15, 19
24 2 Kings 9.27
25 2 Chron. 35.20–24 cf. 2 Kings 23.28–30
26 Ps. 48.1, 2; 125.2
27 In fact, only in Josh. 11.5, 7
28 For 'Chinnereth' see Num. 34.11 and Deut. 3.17; for 'Gennesaret' Lk. 5.1
29 2 Kings 5.12
30 Jer. 49.19
31 Mk. 1.5
32 cf. Ezek. 47.1–12
33 Gen. 19.24–29
34 1 Kings 9.26
35 1 Kings 10.22 cf. v.11
36 Josh. 18.7
37 Gen. 32.22–32
38 pp. 217–251
39 Ezek. 39.18 cf. Ps. 22.12
40 Gen. 37.25 cf. Jer. 8.22
41 p. 237
42 2 Kings 3.4
43 Deut. 32.49, 50; 34.1–8; Num. 22.1
44 Num. 20.14–21; 21.4

45 Ps. 80.1; Is. 40.11
46 Ps. 23.1, 2
47 John 10.1–18; Lk. 15.3–7
48 Deut. 7.13; Ps. 104.15;
   Joel 2.19 cf. Hos. 2.8
49 Mic. 4.4
50 Acts 14. 15–17; Mt. 5.45
51 1 Sam. 12.16–18; Prov.
   26.1
52 Hos. 13.3
53 p. 79
54 Deut. 28.23
55 Lk. 9.62

56 Jn. 4.35; Joel 3.13
57 cf. Is. 41.15
58 e.g. Ps. 1.4; Lk. 3.17
59 Jer. 5.24
60 Deut. 11.13, 14
61 Jas. 5.7
62 Ps. 65.9–13
63 Deut. 16.12
64 Lev. 23.39–43
65 Ex. 23.14–17 cf. Deut.
   16.16, 17
66 Deut. 26.1–11

3. THE STORY OF THE BIBLE
(OLD TESTAMENT)

Christianity is essentially a historical religion. God's revelation, which Christians cherish and seek to communicate, was not given in a vacuum but in an unfolding historical situation, through a nation called Israel and a person called Jesus Christ. It must never be divorced from its historical context; it can be understood only within it.

This does not mean that the history recorded in the Bible is identical in every respect with the modern view of history. A historian today is supposed to give a full and objective account of all the facts of his period. The Biblical historians, however, made no such claim. On the contrary, they were regarded as 'the former prophets', for they were writing 'sacred history', the story of God's dealings with a particular people, for a particular purpose. They were convinced that God had 'not dealt thus with any other nation'.[1] So their record is more a testimony than a history. They were writing down their own confession of faith.

Therefore, they were selective in their choice of material and (the secular historian would add) unbalanced in their presentation of it. For example, ancient Babylonia, Persia, Egypt, Greece and Rome—each a mighty empire and a rich civilisation—are only included as they impinge on the fortunes of Israel and Judah, two tiny buffer states on the edge of the Arabian desert, which hardly anybody had heard of. The great thinkers of Greece like Aristotle, Socrates and Plato are not so much as mentioned, nor are national heroes like Alexander the Great (except obliquely) and Julius Caesar.

Instead, the scriptural record concentrates on men like Abraham, Moses, David, Isaiah and the prophets to whom the word of God came, and on Jesus Christ, God's Word made flesh. For the concern of Scripture is not with the wisdom, wealth or might of the world, but with the salvation of God. Biblical history is *Heilsgeschichte*, the story of salvation.

The sweep of this sacred history is magnificent. Although it omits great areas of human civilisation which would feature prominently in any history of the world written by men, yet in principle and from God's point of view it tells the whole story of man from start to finish, from the beginning when 'God created the heavens and the earth' to the end when He will create 'a new heaven and a new earth'.[2]

Christians divide history into B.C. and A.D., before Christ and after Christ, believing that Jesus Christ's coming into the world is the watershed of history. So too it is the life of Jesus Christ which divides the Bible into half, the Old Testament looking forward to His arrival and preparing for it, the New Testament telling the story of His life, death and resurrection and drawing out its implications as they began to emerge in the infant church and will one day reach fruition.

In this chapter I shall attempt to give an outline of the story of the Old Testament, and in the following chapter its sequel in the New Testament. Then, having looked at the Bible's geographical and historical setting, we shall be ready in chapter 5 to consider the message which God chose to give in it.

The Old Testament is a library of thirty-nine books. The order in which they are placed[3] is dictated neither by the date of their composition, nor even by the date of the subject matter they contain, but by their literary genre. Broadly speaking, there are three types of literature in the Old Testament: history, poetry and prophecy. The historical books (the five from Genesis to Deuteronomy forming the 'Pentateuch' and then twelve more) do tell a continuous story. They begin with the creation of man in Genesis 1 and the call of Abraham in Genesis 12. They go on to tell the story of Israel, the birth of the nation in the rest of the Pentateuch, its varied fortunes during nearly seven centuries in the promised land (in the books of Joshua, Judges, Samuel, Kings and Chronicles), and its rebirth under the leadership of Ezra and Nehemiah. After these seventeen historical books come five books of Hebrew poetry or 'Wisdom'—Job, Psalms, Proverbs, Ecclesiastes and the Song of Solomon—and finally the seventeen prophetical books, five 'major' prophets (Isaiah, Jeremiah, Lamentations, Ezekiel and Daniel) and twelve 'minor' ones (from Hosea to Malachi).

Any reconstruction of the Old Testament story is bound to be somewhat arbitrary. Scholars are still debating, for example, the date of the Exodus and the order in which Ezra and Nehemiah left their Babylonian exile in the 5th century in order to visit Jerusalem. I propose to tell the story according to what I believe is the consensus of most conservative scholars.

The Creation

The Bible begins with a majestic account of the creation of the universe, of earth, of life and of man. It establishes from the outset that the God who later chose to reveal Himself to Israel was not the God of Israel alone. Israel must not regard Yahweh[4] as the Moabites regarded Chemosh and the Ammonites their god Milcom or Molech, almost as a national mascot. For He was no petty godling or tribal deity whose domain and interests were limited to the tribe and its territory, but the God of creation, the Lord of the whole earth.

It is true that the Genesis account of creation is earth-centred and man-centred, in the sense that it is deliberately told from the perspective of man upon earth, but it is above all God-centred in the sense that the whole initiative in the creation lies with the one, true God:

'In the beginning God created . . . and God said . . . and God saw . . . and God called . . . and God blessed . . . and God finished . . .'.

This simple, unadorned narrative, which ascribes wisdom, purpose, power and goodness to the creator God, is far removed from the fantastic and even disgusting creation stories which emanate from the ancient Near East. There are superficial similarities, in that both begin with chaos and end with some kind of cosmos. But the dissimilarities are greater. The Near-Eastern stories are crude, polytheistic, immoral and grotesque; the Biblical account is dignified, monotheistic, ethical and sublime.

The creation story of Genesis 1 begins with God ('in the beginning God created . . .'), continues with progressive stages ('and God said . . .') and ends with man ('so

God created man in his own image'). Not many Christians today imagine that the 'days' of creation were intended to be understood as precise periods of twenty-four hours each. Indeed, speaking for myself, I cannot see that at least some forms of the theory of evolution contradict or are contradicted by the Genesis revelation. Scripture reveals religious truths about God, that He created all things by His word, that His creation was 'good', and that His creative programme culminated in man; science suggests that 'evolution' may have been the mode which God employed in creating.[5]

To suggest this tentatively need not in any way detract from man's uniqueness. I myself believe in the historicity of Adam and Eve, as the original couple from whom the human race is descended. I shall give my reasons in chapter 7, when I come to the question of how we are to interpret Scripture. But my acceptance of Adam and Eve as historical is not incompatible with my belief that several forms of pre-Adamic 'hominid' may have existed for thousands of years previously. These hominids began to advance culturally. They made their cave drawings and buried their dead. It is conceivable that God created Adam out of one of them. You may call them *homo erectus.* I think you may even call some of them *homo sapiens,* for these are arbitrary scientific names. But Adam was the first *homo divinus,* if I may coin the phrase, the first man to whom may be given the Biblical designation 'made in the image of God'. Precisely what the divine likeness was, which was stamped upon him, we do not know, for Scripture nowhere tells us. But Scripture seems to suggest that it included rational, moral, social and spiritual faculties which make man unlike all other creatures and like God the creator, and on account of which he was given 'dominion' over the lower creation.

When shall we date Adam, then? The chronology which was added in 1701 to the Authorized Version of the Bible (1611) was calculated by James Ussher, Archbishop of Armagh, from the Biblical genealogies. By working backwards he reckoned that Adam was created in the year 4004 B.C. But the genealogies never claim to be complete. For example, it is written in one of the genealogies of Jesus that Joram 'begat' Uzziah, whereas we know from the Second Book of Kings that he was actually not his father but his great-great-grandfather. Three complete generations have been left out. And recent Near-Eastern studies have confirmed that such omissions were a regular practice in genealogies.

The text itself gives us some better clues. The Biblical account of Adam and his immediate descendants in Genesis 3 and 4 seems to imply a Neolithic civilisation. Adam is said to have been put in a garden to 'till it and keep it'. His sons Cain and Abel are described as having been respectively 'a tiller of the ground' and 'a keeper of sheep', while Cain's son Enoch 'built a city', which may not have been more than a fairly rudimentary village. These are significant expressions, since farming the land and domesticating animals (as opposed to foraging and hunting), together with primitive community life in villages, did not begin until the late Stone Age. Only a few generations later we read of those who played 'the lyre and pipe' and those who forged 'instruments of bronze and iron'. Since the Neolithic age is usually dated from about 6,000 B.C., this would still suggest a comparatively late date for Adam.

The second chapter of Genesis tells us that work and leisure (six days' work and one day's rest), and monogamous marriage, are 'creation ordinances' instituted by God for man's benefit before sin entered the world. The entry of sin through man's 'fall' or disobedience is described in Genesis 3, and in the following chapters the resulting deterioration of man and his society, and the inevitable judgments of God. The flood seems to have been a comparatively local disaster. It is recorded as an object lesson of God's judgment on human wickedness and of His mercy both towards Noah's family and towards all subsequent generations in His solemn covenant that 'while the earth remains, seedtime and harvest, cold and heat, summer and winter, day and night, shall not cease'.[6] Similarly, the building of the tower of Babel, which may have been a Babylonian *ziggurat*[7] or something similar, is recorded as an example of divine judgment on human pride, leading to the scattering of the nations.[8]

God's Promise to Abraham

It was some time after the year 2,000 B.C. that a new beginning of immense importance took place with God's call of Abraham. It seems to have come to him first in Ur of the Chaldees, then in Haran. It summoned him to leave his country and his kindred in exchange for another country and another kindred which God would later give him:

> 'Now the Lord said to Abram, "Go from your country and your kindred and your father's house to the land that I will show you. And I will make of you a great nation, and I will bless you, and make your name great, so that you will be a blessing. I will bless those who bless you, and him who curses you I will curse; and in you all the families of the earth will be blessed".'[9]

Fundamentally, God's promise was 'I will bless you'. This was spelled out later:

> 'I will establish My covenant between Me and you . . . to be God to you and to your descendants after you'.[10]

It came to be recognized as the essence of God's covenant with Israel, repeated again and again in the Old Testament 'I will be your God and you shall be My people'. In addition to this covenant-relationship God promised Abraham both a land and a seed. It may truly be said without exaggeration that not only the rest of the Old Testament but the whole of the New Testament are an outworking of these promises of God. In Old Testament days Israel was the promised seed and Canaan the promised land. But the covenant included a reference to 'all the families of the earth' and their blessing. Only now in Christ have these promises begun to be fulfilled. For Jesus Christ and His people are the true seed of Abraham. As Paul wrote to the Galatians:

'If you are Christ's, then you are Abraham's offspring, heirs according to promise'.[11]

The final fulfilment lies beyond history. Then Abraham's seed will be 'a great multitude which no man can number', as many in fact as the stars in the sky and the sand on the seashore, and their inheritance will be the new Jerusalem, 'the city which has foundations, whose builder and maker is God'.[12]

God kept renewing His covenant to Abraham during his lifetime, and then confirmed it to his son Isaac and to his grandson Jacob.[13] The Palestine of their day was in the Bronze Age, but they never settled down to enjoy it. They were nomads. The only territory they possessed was a field near Hebron, which Abraham bought so that he could bury his wife Sarah in its cave.[14]

Jacob (whose other name was 'Israel') had twelve sons. They were, in fact, the original 'children of Israel'. But these progenitors of Israel's twelve tribes all spent their declining years and died not in the promised land of Canaan, but in Egypt, to which famine had driven them. Joseph had become a very senior administrator in Egypt, perhaps even a kind of grand vizier. Such a promotion is not as improbable as some have thought, for the ruling

Egyptian dynasty from about 1700 B.C. were the Hyksos, the so-called shepherd-kings, who were themselves Semitic in origin. But Joseph also died in exile, and the Book of Genesis ends with the statement:

'they embalmed him, and he was put in a coffin in Egypt'.[15]

When the bald statement is made in Exodus 1.8 that 'there arose a new king over Egypt, who did not know Joseph', one of the succeeding dynasties is meant. This is likely to have been the nineteenth, whose early Pharaohs built the cities Pithom and Raamses, the latter as a royal residence in the Delta area, where the Israelites had settled. It was convenient, therefore, to use Israelite slave labour.[16] And as the years passed, the bondage of the Israelites became crueller and harder to bear, until their lives became 'bitter with hard service, in mortar and brick, and in all kinds of work in the field'.[17]

The Egyptian exile lasted altogether 430 years.[18] What had become of God's promise?

The Exodus from Egypt

As the people of Israel groaned under the Pharaohs' oppressive régime, they cried to God for deliverance:

'And God heard their groaning, and God remembered His covenant with Abraham, with Isaac, and with Jacob.'[19]

Indeed, already God was preparing the deliverer He had chosen. By a remarkable providence Moses had actually been brought up in the Egyptian court and learned 'all the wisdom of the Egyptians'.[20] But he had had to flee for his life and was now in hiding in the Sinai peninsula.[21] Here, near Mt. Horeb (or Sinai), where he would later receive the ten commandments for the new-born nation, God spoke to him from the burning bush:

'I am the God of your father, the God of Abraham, the God of Isaac, and the God of Jacob'.[22]

Then God told Moses that He was about to rescue the people of Israel from their bondage and bring them at last into the land of promise. He further commissioned Moses to go to Pharaoh and demand His people's release.

At first Moses was full of apprehension. He was frightened of Pharaoh, and even more of the response he might get from his fellow-Israelites. But God reassured him:

'Say this to the people of Israel, "The Lord, the God of your fathers, the God of Abraham, the God of Isaac, and the God of Jacob, has sent me to you".'[23]

Moses obeyed. And the people of Israel accepted his leadership. But Pharaoh, probably Rameses II who reigned over Egypt for sixty-six years (1290–1224), demurred. In Biblical language he 'hardened his heart'. Not until the ten plagues had decisively demonstrated Yahweh's superiority over all the gods of Egypt did he finally consent.[24] The date will have been about 1280 B.C.

'The Red Sea' which the escaping Israelites crossed was probably some shallow water north of the northern tip of the Suez Gulf. The miracle lay not in the 'strong east wind' which parted the waters, but in the fact that God sent it at the very moment when 'Moses stretched out his hand over the sea'.[25]

Israel never forgot their safe exodus from Egypt by the supernatural intervention of God. They sang of it in public worship as a signal example of God's power and mercy:

He saved them for His name's sake,
    that He might make known His mighty power.

He rebuked the Red Sea, and it became dry;
and He led them through the deep as through a
desert.
So He saved them from the hand of the foe,
and delivered them from the power of the enemy.[26]

O give thanks to the Lord, for He is good,
for His steadfast love endures for ever.
O give thanks to the God of gods,
for His steadfast love endures for ever;
to Him who smote the first-born of Egypt,
for His steadfast love endures for ever;
and brought Israel out from among them,
for His steadfast love endures for ever;
with a strong hand and an outstretched arm,
for His steadfast love endures for ever;
to Him who divided the Red Sea in sunder,
for His steadfast love endures for ever;
and made Israel pass through the midst of it,
for His steadfast love endures for ever.

The escaping Israelites, a large and ragged multitude, did not travel direct to the promised land along the coastal route known as 'The Way of the Land of the Philistines'. They turned south-east to meet their God at Mt. Sinai, as He had directed Moses. It took them about three months to get there, and once encamped at the foot of the mountain they stayed almost a year.

Here God gave Israel three precious gifts—a renewed covenant, a moral law and atoning sacrifices.

The renewal of the covenant came first. God told Moses up the mountain to say to Israel:

'You have seen what I did to the Egyptians, and how I bore you on eagles' wings and brought you to Myself. Now therefore, if you will obey My voice and keep My covenant, you shall be My own possession among all peoples; for all the earth is Mine, and you shall be to Me a kingdom of priests and a holy nation.'[28]

Secondly, God gave Israel a moral law. Obedience to this law was to be Israel's part in the covenant. Its essence was the ten commandments. But these were supplemented both by further 'statutes' ('you shall', 'you shall not') and by 'judgments' which form a body of case-law ('when a man . . .'). The covenant was solemnly ratified by the blood of sacrifice when the people gave a public undertaking to keep God's law.

Thirdly, God made generous provision for breaches of His law. He gave instructions for the building of a 'tabernacle', a rectangular tent measuring about forty-five feet by fifteen, made of dyed linen curtains stretched over a frame and covered with goats' hair and waterproof skins. Inside were two rooms, 'the holy place' and 'the most holy place' or 'holy of holies'. This inner sanctuary was half the size of the bigger room, from which it was separated by a curtain known as 'the veil'. Outside the veil stood a golden lampstand, an incense altar and a table on which baked cakes were displayed. Beyond the veil was the sacred ark, a wooden chest containing the stone tablets on which the ten commandments were inscribed. Its golden lid, called the 'mercy seat', was flanked by cherubim, figures of celestial creatures. In heathen temples these would have formed a kind of throne for the idol. But not in Israel's tabernacle, since the making of idols was forbidden. Instead, God manifested Himself here in a kind of radiance. This was 'the Shekinah', His abiding presence in the midst of His people.[29]

The tabernacle was pitched in a large courtyard. Outside its east-facing door stood a copper basin called the laver, where the priests washed their hands and feet, and the great altar on which the animal sacrifices were burned.

The tabernacle's fabric, furniture and construction are described in Exodus 25–27 and 35–40. The five standard sacrifices are explained in Leviticus 1–7, and full details for the dress, consecration and duties of the priests are given in Exodus 28, 29 and the rest of the Book of Leviticus.

Specially significant is the ritual prescribed for the annual Day of Atonement.[30] The high priest was instructed to take two goats. He was to kill one as a sin offering, to take some of its blood 'within the veil' and sprinkle it on the mercy seat. The blood stood for a life laid down in place of the sinner whose life was forfeit:

'For the life of the flesh is in the blood; and I have given it for you upon the altar to make atonement for your souls; for it is the blood that makes atonement, by reason of the life.'[31]

The veil symbolizing God's inaccessibility to the sinner was to be penetrated on no other day than the Day of Atonement, by no other person than the high priest, and on no other condition than the shedding and the sprinkling of blood. Then:

'Aaron shall lay both his hands on the head of the live goat, confess over him all the iniquities of the people of Israel, and all their transgressions, all their sins; and he shall put them upon the head of the goat, and send him away into the wilderness. . . . The goat shall bear all their iniquities upon him to a solitary land . . .'[32]

These symbolic acts—the shedding and sprinkling of blood, the penetration of the veil and the bearing of sin —all prefigure the atoning work of Jesus Christ our Saviour.

The tabernacle was erected on the first anniversary of the Israelites' escape from Egypt.[33] A fortnight later the Passover was celebrated,[34] and a fortnight later still a census taken of all the men of 20 years or more, who would be fit to fight.[35] The development is striking. Israel is seen first as a disorganized rabble of freed slaves,[36] then as a holy nation in covenant with Yahweh,[37] a 'kingdom of priests' among whom He dwelt, but now (in Numbers) as fighting soldiers, an army encamped in battle array, ready to march to the promised land.

On the twentieth day of the second month of the second year the march began. The tabernacle was dismantled, only seven weeks after it had been erected. The pillar of cloud, symbol of God's guiding presence, began to move, 'and the people of Israel set out by stages from the wilderness of Sinai'.[38]

It must have been an exciting moment. At last, seven centuries after it had been first made to Abraham, God's promise to give His people the land of Canaan was about to be fulfilled. 'We are setting out', they said to one another, 'for the place of which the Lord said "I will give it to you" '.[39]

But their expectation was short-lived. First, the people complained about the shortage of food. Their mouth watered for the fish, the cucumbers, melons, leeks, onions and garlic they had enjoyed in Egypt.[40] Then Miriam and Aaron, Moses' sister and brother, began to undermine his authority.[41] Finally, the twelve scouts whom Moses sent out to reconnoitre the land of Canaan, although the fruit they brought back proved that it was indeed 'a land flowing with milk and honey', added that in their view its inhabitants were invincible:

'The people who dwell in the land are strong, and the

cities are fortified and very large ... The Amalekites dwell in the land of the Negeb; the Hittites, the Jebusites, and the Amorites, dwell in the hill country; and the Canaanites dwell by the sea, and along the Jordan. ... We are not able to go up against the people; for they are stronger than we.'[42]

At this report the people wept and wailed. Two of the spies, Caleb and Joshua, pleaded with them not to disobey or disbelieve the Lord or fear the people of the land. But all to no avail. The majority spoke only of stoning them. So God's judgment fell upon His people for their inveterate rebellion. None of that adult generation would enter the land of promise, He said. Only the faithful Caleb and Joshua.

Forty years were now to elapse between the exodus from Egypt and the entry into Canaan, instead of only one or two. Many of them seem to have been spent at the oasis of Kadesh-barnea in the Negeb. But they were years of wandering, too, down south to Sinai again, then north and east through rugged Edomite territory south of the Dead Sea. From here they could have joined the famous 'King's Highway' which ran from the gulf of Aqabah east of the Dead Sea right up into Syria. But the Edomites would not allow them to traverse their territory by this route, so they had to skirt round it farther east.[43] They did not fight the Edomites, for they were kinsmen. But north of them now were the Amorites, also blocking the King's Highway, under Sihon King of Heshbon and Og King of Bashan. Their defeat in battle, and the defeat of the King of Moab's attempts to overthrow Israel, first by hiring Balaam to curse them and then by immoral enticement, are described in Numbers 21–25.

Israel was now encamped on the plains of Moab close to the River Jordan north of where it flows into the Dead Sea. Here Moses gave the people his final charge, preserved in the Book of Deuteronomy. He began by recalling the recent years of tragic wandering and its solemn lessons. He then reminded them of the Lord's covenant and of its conditions. He rehearsed the ten commandments and expounded them in terms of Israel's requirement to love the Lord their God with all their being and to prove their love by their obedience.

'You are a people holy to the Lord your God; the Lord your God has chosen you to be a people for His own possession, out of all the peoples that are on the face of the earth . . . And now, Israel, what does the Lord your God require of you, but to fear the Lord your God, to walk in all His ways, to love Him, to serve the Lord your God with all your heart and with all your soul, and to keep the commandments and statutes of the Lord. . . .?'[44]

Moses went on to expound a number of laws in detail, applying them to the situation the people might expect in the promised land. Two or three times in the course of his exposition he placed before the Israelites the only alternatives:

'Behold, I set before you this day a blessing and a curse: the blessing, if you obey the commandments of the Lord your God . . ., and the curse, if you do not obey the commandments of the Lord your God . . . See, I have set before you this day life and good, death and evil . . .'[45]

The death of Moses is recorded at the end of Deuteronomy. For forty years he had served God and the people of God with extraordinary patience and faithfulness. He had acted as lawgiver, administrator and judge. Above all he was a chosen spokesman of God, a prophet. Indeed the writer adds:

'And there has not arisen a prophet since in Israel like Moses, whom the Lord knew face to face.'[46]

Israel's Settlement in Canaan

Already, before his death, Moses by divine command had appointed Joshua to succeed him and to lead the people into the promised land. Now therefore God's word came to Joshua:

'Be strong and of good courage; for you shall cause this people to inherit the land which I swore to their fathers to give them.'[47]

The Israelites were able to cross the river Jordan, as they had crossed the Red Sea, by a supernatural act of God, although this time He seems to have used a landslide instead of a strong wind to stem the waters for them.[48] Before them stood the ancient walled city of Jericho; its destruction without a siege was their first victory in the land of promise. After an initial defeat at Ai, owing to the disobedience of Achan in stealing loot, the victorious Israelites turned south. They routed a confederate army led by five Amorite kings, and swept on to conquer the southern hill country up to the borders of Philistia.

Next they turned north, where a coalition commanded by Jabin King of Hazor had gathered near Lake Huleh. Although this army was equipped with 'very many horses and chariots', for Israel's settlement in Canaan coincided approximately with the beginning of the Iron Age, it too was decisively defeated:

'So Joshua took all that land, the hill country and all the Negeb and all the land of Goshen and the lowland and the Arabah and the hill country of Israel and its lowland from Mount Halak, that rises toward Seir, as

far as Baalgad in the valley of Lebanon below Mount
Hermon . . .'[49]

The rest of the Book of Joshua contains a description
of the territories which were allocated by lot to the
Israelite tribes as their inheritance (chapters 13–22). It
ends with a stirring speech which Joshua delivered 'a
long time afterward', reminiscent of Moses' charge
recorded in Deuteronomy, in which he reminded the
people of their history and issued this challenge:

'Now therefore fear the Lord, and serve Him in sincerity and in faithfulness; put away the gods which
your fathers served beyond the River, and in Egypt,
and serve the Lord. And if you be unwilling to serve
the Lord, choose this day whom you will serve,
whether the gods your fathers served in the region
beyond the River, or the gods of the Amorites in
whose land you dwell; but as for me and my house, we
will serve the Lord.'[50]

Although the children of Israel were now settled in the
land which God had promised to give them, they had
not obeyed His command to exterminate its former
inhabitants. There is no need for us to be offended by this
divine decree. The reason for it can best be described as
the need for radical surgery. Canaanite religion was
characterized by both idolatry and immorality of the
worst kind. The 'baals' were fertility gods, supposed to
be responsible for rainfall and harvest, and both ritual
prostitution and sexual orgies defiled the 'worship' of
the local sanctuaries. So Moses said:

'It is because of the wickedness of these nations that
the Lord is driving them out before you.'[51]

Indeed so degraded were the practices of the heathen
nations inhabiting Canaan, including the abomination of

child sacrifice, that their ejection by Israel is sometimes portrayed in Scripture as the land 'vomiting out its inhabitants'.[52]

Israel's failure to obey God's command resulted in the persistence of heathen culture within her territory and its penetration into her beliefs and practices. This is the situation throughout the period—nearly 200 years—described in the Book of Judges. The same cycle of backsliding, oppression and deliverance kept repeating itself. First the backsliding:

'And the people of Israel did what was evil in the sight of the Lord and served the Baals; and they forsook the Lord, the God of their fathers, who had brought them out of the land of Egypt; they went after other gods, from among the gods of the peoples who were round about them, and bowed down to them; and they provoked the Lord to anger. They forsook the Lord, and served the Baals and the Ashtaroth.'[53]

Then came the judgment in form of a foreign oppression:

'So the anger of the Lord was kindled against Israel, and He gave them over to plunderers, who plundered them; and He sold them into the power of their enemies round about, so that they could no longer withstand their enemies.'[54]

Finally the deliverance:

'Then the Lord raised up judges, who saved them out of the power of those who plundered them.'[55]

But then it happened all over again:

'And yet they did not listen to their judges; for they played the harlot after other gods and bowed down to them; they soon turned aside from the way in which their fathers had walked, who had obeyed the commandments of the Lord, and they did not do so.'[56]

These 'judges' combined several functions. First and foremost they were military leaders, raised up to deliver Israel from her oppressors. Thus Ehud rescued Israel from the Moabites, Deborah from the Canaanites, Gideon from the Midianites, Jephthah from the Amorites and Samson from the Philistines. Next they were spiritual leaders, men of the Spirit, though exhibiting different degrees of devotion to Yahweh. Thirdly, they were judges, as their title indicates, hearing cases referred to them and administering justice in Israel. Nevertheless, there appears to have been but little law and order throughout this period, which is well summed up by the last words of the book:

'Every man did what was right in his own eyes.'

Undoubtedly the greatest of the judges was Samuel. Unlike the others he displayed no military prowess. It was during his term of office that the unthinkable disaster occurred: the Philistines captured the ark of God and transferred it from Shiloh to Ashdod. Samuel relied on spiritual weapons to recover it—prayer and national repentance.

His reputation as a spiritual leader began early. Dedicated to the Lord before his birth, he was brought up at Shiloh under the tutelage of the high priest Eli. Already when he was a young man, we are told, 'all Israel from Dan to Beersheba knew that Samuel was established as a prophet of the Lord'.[57] He acted as a priest as well.

He also judged Israel, going on circuit every year from Ramah, his home town, to Bethel, Gilgal and Mizpah.[58]

However, when he grew old and appointed his sons as judges, they did not walk in their father's ways, but 'took bribes and perverted justice'.[59] So the elders of Israel came to Samuel at Ramah and demanded that he should appoint a king to govern them. As Samuel prayed about their request, it became clear to him that they had rejected not him but God. For Israel had been a theocracy, a nation ruled by God, since its beginning some 250 years before. Therefore Samuel remonstrated with them and warned them that future kings would oppress them. But the people refused to listen and said:

'No! but we will have a king over us, that we also may be like all the nations. . . .'[60]

The Establishment of the Monarchy

Israel's first king, Saul the son of Kish, began his reign with great promise. He was rich, tall, handsome, young and popular. He was also a strong patriot, so that when he heard that Jabesh-gilead was being besieged by Nahash the Ammonite he immediately mustered a large army and made a bold dash across the Jordan to rescue them.

He was not so successful against the Philistines, however. They had garrisons on Israelite territory and were a source of constant humiliation to Israel. It was Saul's son Jonathan who one day routed a whole Philistine garrison single-handed, and the youth David (destined to be Saul's successor on the throne) who slew the Philistine giant Goliath. The people were enthusiastic over these daring exploits. But Saul's jealousy was aroused.

The major cause of Saul's downfall was his disobedience. Three times he disobeyed the plain commands of God—in not utterly destroying the Amalekites, in usurping the priestly prerogative of sacrifice and in consulting a medium. God's verdict through Samuel was inevitable:

'Because you have rejected the word of the Lord, He has also rejected you from being king'.[61]

Saul fell in battle against the Philistines, together with his three sons, and David was overcome with grief:

'Thy glory, O Israel, is slain upon thy high places! How are the mighty fallen!'[62]

David had already been designated heir to the throne during Saul's lifetime, but spent the latter years of Saul's reign a fugitive from the king's jealousy. He began his own reign in Hebron, where the men of Judah (his own tribe) anointed him king. But, seven years later, representatives of all the tribes of Israel came to Hebron to do homage to him, and he was anointed king for the second time. He then moved his capital to Jebus (captured only now from the Jebusites), changed its name to Jerusalem, 'city of peace', and brought the ark there from Kiriath-jearim amid tumultuous rejoicing.

David's first achievement was to unify Israel and make the country safe from her enemies. He won victories over all Israel's traditional foes—the Philistines, Edomites, Moabites, Ammonites and Syrians—and ruled over the whole promised land from 'the river of Egypt' (Egypt's frontier wadi) to the River Euphrates. In view of these conquests it was all the more humiliating that he should have to endure rebellion at home, first from his son Absalom and then from a worthless pretender named Sheba.

But David was far from being a war lord. He was artistic, being both a poet and a musician (he had often soothed Saul's melancholia with his lyre). He was also a sensitive spirit, magnanimous to his enemies and loyal to his friends.

Above all, he was devoted to his God. The psalms he wrote express a remarkable depth of spirituality, of penitence after his adultery with Bathsheba[63] and of trust in the God of his salvation. For example:

'The Lord is my rock, and my fortress, and my
    deliverer,
my God, my rock, in whom I take refuge,
my shield and the horn of my salvation,
    my stronghold and my refuge,
my saviour; Thou savest me from violence.' ...

'For who is God, but the Lord?
    And who is a rock, except our God?
This God is my strong refuge, and has made my way
    safe.'

'I love thee, O Lord, my strength.
The Lord is my rock, and my fortress, and my
    deliverer,
my God, my rock, in whom I take refuge,
my shield, and the horn of my salvation, my
    stronghold.

I call upon the Lord, who is worthy to be praised,
and I am saved from my enemies. . . .
For who is God, but the Lord,
And who is a rock, except our God?—
the God who girded me with strength, and made my
  way safe.'[64]

Having built a palace for himself in Jerusalem, David
was anxious also to build a house for the Lord. But
through the prophet Nathan God forbade it, telling him
that his son would be allowed to build the temple.
Meanwhile God added:

'Moreover the Lord declares to you that the Lord will
make you a house . . ., and your house and your
kingdom shall be made sure for ever before Me; your
throne shall be established for ever.'[65]

Israel never forgot God's everlasting covenant with
David. Believers in Israel knew for certain that when
Messiah came, He would be a son of David.

God began to fulfil His promise to David by setting his
son Solomon on the throne, and during his reign the
kingdom of Israel reached the zenith of its magnificence.
It was not for nothing that Jesus referred to 'Solomon in
all his glory'.

King Solomon had a genius for administration and
building. Soon after his accession he prayed that God
would give him wisdom:

'Give Thy servant . . . an understanding mind to govern
thy people, that I may discern between good and
evil . . .'[66]

Solomon's prayer was answered. He divided the country
into twelve regions under twelve officers, whose responsibility was to make provision for the royal household,
one each month of the year. He fortified cities, built up a

standing army, and provided himself with 1,400 chariots and 40,000 horses. He was the father of Israel's navy, whose ships (kept in the Gulf of Aqabah) embarked on adventurous voyages for trade. He built palaces for himself and his queen, halls for assembly, justice and armoury and above all the great Temple, made of hewn stone, cedar and cypress wood and gold. He was also a kind of patron of the arts, and himself the author of numerous songs and proverbs.[67] His reputation for splendour, wisdom and justice spread far and wide, and under his rule his people enjoyed peace and prosperity:

'Judah and Israel were as many as the sand by the sea; they ate and drank and were happy . . .
And Judah and Israel dwelt in safety, from Dan even to Beersheba, every man under his vine and under his fig tree . . .'.[68]

All was not as well as it seemed on the surface, however. Solomon did not love the Lord his God with all his heart. Nor did he love his neighbour as himself. He kept a harem of foreign (heathen) princesses, in defiance of God's prohibition of such intermarriage, and they 'turned away his heart after other gods'.[69] And he was able to maintain his building programme and his grandiose life-style at court only by oppressive measures, including high taxation and a levy of forced labour numbering 30,000 men.

It is not surprising, therefore, that when the people came together to make Rehoboam king in succession to his father Solomon, they said to him:

'Your father made our yoke heavy. Now therefore lighten the hard service of your father and his heavy yoke upon us, and we will serve you'.[70]

The old king's counsellors gave Rehoboam wise advice,

which lies at the foundation of every modern constitutional monarchy's ideals of service:

'If you will be a servant to this people today and serve them, . . . then they will be your servants for ever'.[71]

But Rehoboam made a rash and foolish mistake. He accepted instead the advice of young and inexperienced counsellors, warned the people that he intended to add to their yoke, and so provoked the ten northern and eastern tribes to proclaim their independence of the dynasty of David.

Saul, David and Solomon had reigned over all Israel for forty years each, so that for the 120 years from approximately 1050–930 B.C. there had been a united kingdom. But now the kingdom was divided. The northern kingdom was Israel, with Jeroboam its first king and its capital city Shechem (later changed to Samaria). The southern kingdom was Judah, with Rehoboam its first king and its capital city Jerusalem. Israel had several changes of dynasty and lasted just over 200 years until the destruction of Samaria in 722 B.C. Judah was more stable, retaining the dynasty of David throughout its longer history of about 350 years until Jerusalem was destroyed in 586 B.C.

The story of the divided monarchy is not easy to follow, as we try to understand the relations between the two kingdoms, their involvement with the mighty empires to their north and south, and the intervention of the prophets who spoke boldly in the name of Yahweh to kings and commoners alike. The Biblical story is further complicated by the fact that much of it is told twice, once in the Books of Kings and once in the Books of Chronicles, the chronicler (? Ezra) writing later with the clear object of emphasizing the importance of the southern kingdom, the Davidic dynasty and the temple cultus. It may be best to concentrate first on the story of Israel.

The Northern Kingdom of Israel

Jeroboam, the first ruler of the northern kingdom, had been one of Solomon's servants. Indeed, so high an opinion did Solomon form of his ability and industry that he put him in charge of a major part of the forced labour levy. Later Solomon had reason to suspect Jeroboam of treason, and Jeroboam fled for his life to Egypt where he was harboured by Shishak (= Sheshonq I of the XXII Dynasty). He only returned after Solomon's death to challenge Rehoboam, as we have seen.

In order to wean the hearts of his subjects from the house of David, Jeroboam was determined to stop them going on pilgrimage to Jerusalem. So he made two alternative sanctuaries, the one up north at Dan and the other down south at Bethel, installed in each a golden calf, and said:

'Behold your gods, O Israel, who brought you up out of the land of Egypt'.[72]

It is for this reason that Jeroboam has gone down to posterity as the one 'who made Israel to sin.'

But Judah under Rehoboam was scarcely any better, for alongside the worship of Yahweh the people corrupted themselves with some of the abominations of the Canaanite fertility rituals. Rehoboam had only been king for four or five years when Shishak invaded Jerusalem and denuded the temple of the treasures with which Solomon had enriched it.

Jeroboam was succeeded on the throne of Israel by five kings of whom we know little. But in 881 B.C., some 28 years after Jeroboam's death, the dynasty of Omri began. It was he who established his capital in Samaria, and made it almost impregnable on a well fortified conical hill. But he brought great trouble to Israel by marrying his son Ahab (who soon succeeded him) to the Phoenician princess Jezebel. For she was not only herself a worshipper of Melqart ('Baal' in the Biblical narrative), the main deity of Tyre, but insisted on maintaining at her own expense at court a retinue of 'the prophets of Baal', and involved her husband the king in her idolatrous worship. She also killed the prophets of the Lord.

This brazen apostasy in the palace was the signal for the reawakening of ethical prophecy, which was destined to play a dominant part in Israel and Judah for the next three centuries and more. The first prophet of this noble line was Elijah, who came from Gilead in Transjordan. Austere in his private life-style and fearless in his public ministry, he accused Ahab of troubling Israel by his religious defection. He also challenged the prophets of Baal to a public contest on Mt. Carmel, at the same time taunting the people with double-mindedness, 'limping with two different opinions'.[73] When Baal's prophets had failed to elicit any response from their god, Elijah prayed:

'O Lord, God of Abraham, Isaac and Israel, let it be known this day that Thou art God in Israel, and that I am Thy servant'.[74]

The outcome was an incontrovertible vindication of the living God.

Elijah had a social as well as a religious conscience. He knew that Yahweh was as displeased with the king's oppression of his subjects as with his apostasy. Next to a palace which belonged to Ahab on the plain of Jezreel there was a desirable vineyard owned by a man named Naboth. Ahab coveted it for himself, but Naboth refused to sell his fathers' inheritance. So Jezebel, doubtless with

Ahab's connivance, had Naboth assassinated and proceeded to annex his property. Here Elijah met him:

'Have you killed, and also taken possession? . . . In the place where dogs licked up the blood of Naboth shall dogs lick your own blood'.[75]

Naboth's innocent blood was avenged by Jehu, an Israelite army commander who was now anointed king on the authority of the prophet Elisha. With brutal thoroughness he liquidated the house of Ahab and rid the land of Baal worship.

The dynasty of Jehu lasted nearly a hundred years (c. 841–753 B.C.), almost half the total duration of the northern kingdom. During the early years of the dynasty there was virtually continuous war with Syria, which wrested the whole of Transjordan from Jehu. But it began to be recovered by his grandson, and his great grandson Jeroboam II completed the process.

It was under Jeroboam II (782–753 B.C.) that the northern kingdom of Israel reached its zenith of power:

'He restored the border of Israel from the entrance of Hamath as far as the Sea of the Arabah'.[76]

Peace brought prosperity, prosperity luxury, and luxury licence. True, the local sanctuaries were thronged with pilgrims, and to all appearances Israel was experiencing a religious boom. But the prophets had eyes only for the injustice and immorality of the nation's leaders. Amos, the first great prophet of the 8th century B.C.,[77] was a simple shepherd from the south, but the compulsion of God's word drove him into the northern kingdom to denounce Israel's hypocrisy:

'Thus says the Lord: "For three transgressions of Israel, and for four, I will not revoke the punishment; Because they sell the righteous for silver, and the needy for a pair of shoes—

they that trample the head of the poor into the dust
of the earth, and turn aside the way of the afflicted;
a man and his father go in to the same maiden,
so that My holy name is profaned;
they lay themselves down beside every altar
upon garments taken in pledge;
and in the house of their God they drink
the wine of those who have been fined." '[78]

He knew that religion divorced from morality was an
abomination to Yahweh:

'I hate, I despise your feasts, and I take no delight in
your solemn assemblies.
Even though you offer Me your burnt offerings and
cereal offerings, I will not accept them,
and the peace offerings of your fatted beasts I will not
look upon.
Take away from Me the noise of your songs;
to the melody of your harps I will not listen.
But let justice roll down like waters,
and righteousness like an everflowing stream.'[79]

To Hosea the word of the Lord came through the
agony of his wife's unfaithfulness. For Israel had
similarly broken her marriage covenant with Yahweh
and gone after her 'lovers', the baals of the local shrines.
It was not outward religious devotion God wanted from
Israel, but faithfulness to the covenant:

'I desire steadfast love and not sacrifice, the knowledge
of God, rather than burnt offerings'.[80]

When the dynasty of Jehu came to an end, the northern
kingdom had only about thirty years left. A succession of
military rulers occupied the throne. But the new factor in
international politics was the rise of the great Assyrian
empire. Already in the middle of the previous century

both Ahab and Jehu had paid tribute to King Shalmaneser III. Now the King of Assyria was Tiglath-Pileser III (745–727 B.C.), called Pul in the Biblical narrative, and he embarked on a series of expansionist campaigns. When he reached Israel, he was bought off by King Menahem with a thousand talents of silver.

A few years later (in 735 B.C.) the 'colonel' who was ruling Israel, Pekah the son of Remaliah, entered into an alliance with Rezin King of Syria to throw off the Assyrian yoke. When Ahaz King of Judah refused to join them, they invaded his territory. Ahaz was thrown into a panic, but the prophet Isaiah sought to calm him with a word from God:

'Take heed, be quiet, do not fear, and do not let your heart be faint because of these two smouldering stumps of firebrands . . . If you will not believe, surely you shall not be established'.[81]

Ahaz did not believe. Instead, he appealed to Tiglath-Pileser for help, with devastating results. Syria was overthrown. The Galilean and Transjordanian territories of Israel were depopulated. And Ahaz paid homage to Tiglath-Pileser with silver and gold from the temple, and even to Ashur, Assyria's god.

When Tiglath-Pileser died, Samaria defiantly withheld tribute from Assyria. This reckless act sounded Israel's death knell. The new King Shalmaneser V laid siege to Samaria, which capitulated three years later (probably in 722) to his successor Sargon II. The people of Israel were largely deported, and their country was colonized with Syrians and Babylonians. The resulting mixed population was the origin of the Samaritans.

So the northern kingdom came to an ignominious end. It had lasted just over two centuries. Israel had regarded God's covenant as rendering her immune to His judgment, but the prophet Amos had taught otherwise:

'You only have I known of all the families of the earth; therefore I will punish you for all your iniquities'.[82]

The Southern Kingdom of Judah

So far we have been following the rise and fall of the northern kingdom. The Books of Kings and Chronicles also give some account of the southern kingdom during the same period. But its history was not so colourful, and the names of its earlier kings are not so well known, except perhaps for Jehoshaphat, Ahab's contemporary.

Now, however, the southern kingdom was to continue alone for a further 135 years. Its period of independence was ennobled in particular by two great religious reforms. The first was promoted by King Hezekiah, with the encouragement of the prophets Isaiah and Micah. The second reforming king was Josiah, who was encouraged by his distant cousin the prophet Zephaniah and by the young prophet Jeremiah.

At the very beginning of his reign Hezekiah repaired and reopened the temple. Then he resolutely removed from his kingdom all the paraphernalia of Assyrian idolatry which his father Ahaz had introduced.

These reforms were certainly the fruit of the faithful witness of Isaiah and Micah who had been denouncing idolatry, empty ritual and social injustice and calling the people to repentance during both the preceding reigns, while Amos and Hosea were proclaiming God's word to the northern kingdom. Here is one of Micah's great oracles:

'With what shall I come before the Lord, and bow myself before God on high?
Shall I come before Him with burnt offerings, with calves a year old?

Will the Lord be pleased with thousands of rams, with ten thousands of rivers of oil?
Shall I give my first-born for my transgression, the fruit of my body for the sin of my soul?"
He has showed you, O man, what is good; and what does the Lord require of you but to do justice, and to love kindness, and to walk humbly with your God?'[83]

Sargon King of Assyria was killed in action in 705 B.C. and succeeded by his son Sennacherib. This seems to have been the signal for Hezekiah's revolt against Assyrian suzerainty. Not until 701 B.C., however, did Sennacherib reach the rebel kingdom of Judah. Having taken its fortified cities, he laid siege to Jerusalem, shutting Hezekiah up (to use his own expression) 'like a bird in a cage'. Fortunately, Hezekiah had taken the precaution of securing the city's water supply by building his famous tunnel from a spring outside the walls to the Pool of Siloam. Even so, the situation appeared desperate. As Isaiah described it:

'The daughter of Zion is left like a booth in a vineyard, like a lodge in a cucumber field, like a besieged city'.[84]

The Assyrian commander taunted the inhabitants of the beleaguered city:

'Do not listen to Hezekiah when he misleads you by saying, "The Lord will deliver us." Has any of the gods of the nations ever delivered his land out of the hand of the King of Assyria? Where are the gods of Hamath and Arpad? Where are the gods of Sepharvaim, Hena, and Ivvah? Have they delivered Samaria out of my hand?'[85]

King Hezekiah consulted Isaiah, and the prophet replied:

'Thus says the Lord: "Do not be afraid because of the

words that you have heard, with which the servants of the King of Assyria have reviled Me." '86

The central doctrine of Isaiah's theology was the sovereignty of God. His call to the prophetic office came to him in a vision of the Lord as a king, reigning from an exalted throne. He believed that God was king of the nations and used them as instruments of His own purpose.

So Sennacherib's siege of Jerusalem was lifted. According to the Biblical record 'that night the angel of the Lord went forth, and slew a hundred and eighty-five thousand in the camp of the Assyrians'.87 It is possible that Herodotus is referring to this incident when he describes a night invasion of the Assyrian camp by field-mice. But he says the mice rendered the soldiers defenceless by eating their bowstrings, quivers and shield-straps, whereas in reality they may rather have been carriers of bubonic plague.

By whatever means it was accomplished, Israel regarded it as an outstanding divine deliverance:

'God is our refuge and strength, a very present help in trouble. . . . "Be still, and know that I am God. I am exalted among the nations, I am exalted in the earth!" The Lord of hosts is with us; the God of Jacob is our refuge.'88

The half-century following Hezekiah's death was a time of religious apostasy. His son Manasseh, an abject vassal of Assyria, adopted a policy of religious syncretism and reintroduced the abominations of Canaanite and Assyrian worship which Hezekiah had destroyed. The astral cult, spiritism, Baal-worship and even the horrors of child-sacrifice defiled the land. Amon his son, who reigned only two years, seems to have been no better.

But good King Josiah who reigned from 639 to 609 B.C., turned the scales again and inaugurated even more thoroughgoing reforms than his great grandfather Hezekiah. He ascended the throne of Judah as a boy of eight. When he was still a youth of sixteen, 'he began to seek the God of David his father', which presumably means that he reformed himself and his immediate entourage at court. Four years later 'he began to purge Judah and Jerusalem of the high places, the Asherim, and the graven and the molten images',[89] and the following year Jeremiah received his call to be a prophet.

It was not until five years later still that, as a young man of twenty-six, Josiah led the radical reform of the whole nation. It was the result of the discovery during repairs in the temple of 'the book of the law', which appears to have been some edition or part of the Book of Deuteronomy. The King summoned the people, 'both great and small', to a large public assembly and himself read to them the rediscovered law-book. He then renewed the nation's covenant with God, had all idolatrous objects of Assyrian and Canaanite worship removed from the city and the provinces, closed down the local sanctuaries, prohibited spiritism and human sacrifice, and ordered the Passover to be celebrated in Jerusalem.

'Before him there was no king like him, who turned to the Lord with all his heart and with all his soul and with all his might, according to all the law of Moses; nor did any like him arise after him.'[90]

We may be sure that, behind the scenes, Jeremiah was encouraging this reformation. At the same time the prophet deplored what he saw to be its comparative superficiality. He drew the people's attention to the fate of faithless Israel, and added:

'Yet for all this her false sister Judah did not return to Me with her whole heart, but in pretence, says the Lord'.[91]

Jeremiah often referred to the 'stubbornness' of men's evil heart, 'deceitful above all things and desperately corrupt', and looked forward to the days of the new covenant when God would put His law within men and 'write it upon their hearts'.[92]

In the event Jeremiah was proved right. The results of Josiah's reform did not last, and his son Jehoiakim quickly succeeded in undoing his good work. The new king seems to have used slave labour to build a luxurious palace for himself, and so brought upon his head one of Jeremiah's fiercest denunciations:

'Woe to him who builds his house by unrighteousness, and his upper rooms by injustice; who makes his neighbour serve him for nothing, and does not give him his wages; who says, "I will build myself a great house with spacious upper rooms," and cuts out windows for it, panelling it with cedar, and painting it with vermilion. Do you think you are a king because you compete in cedar? Did not your father eat and drink and do justice and righteousness? Then it was well with him. He judged the cause of the poor and needy; then it was well. Is not this to know Me? says the Lord. But you have eyes and heart only for your dishonest gain, for shedding innocent blood, and for practising oppression and violence.'[93]

Such outspoken talk was not calculated to establish Jeremiah in King Jehoiakim's favour. So when a scroll containing Jeremiah's warnings of the coming judgment upon Judah was read to the king as he sat in his winter house before a brazier, he cut it up with a penknife and threw it bit by bit into the fire.[94] Jeremiah had to go into hiding.

During these years the international scene underwent some important changes. For the past 200 years the Assyrians had been the dominant power in the Near-

East, and the countryside of Israel and Judah had been repeatedly overrun by their armies. But in 616 B.C. Assyria was invaded by Nabopolasser, the founder of the Babylonian dynasty, and in 612 Nineveh (the Assyrian capital) fell after a siege of two and a half months. No tears were shed over her downfall. The Book of Jonah illustrates how reluctantly an Israelite would contemplate Nineveh's repentance and forgiveness, and the prophet Nahum expresses the widespread reaction to Nineveh's oppression:

> 'Woe to the bloody city, all full of lies and booty—no end to the plunder! . . . Behold I am against you, says the Lord of hosts. . . . All who hear the news of you clap their hands over you. For upon whom has not come your unceasing evil?'[95]

Even after the fall of Nineveh Assyria did not immediately concede defeat. In 609 Pharaoh Necho of Egypt went to her aid, but was himself defeated in 605 by the Babylonians at the Battle of Carchemish on the Euphrates. Now Babylon was supreme, and Judah transferred her homage from Necho to Nebuchadnezzar.

When Nebuchadnezzar's army failed to defeat Necho at the Egyptian border in 601 King Jehoiakim withheld his tribute money. This was tantamount to a rebellion. But Jehoiakim died in 598 before Nebuchadnezzar had had time to quell the revolt, and his son Jehoiachin was left to bear the punitive wrath of Babylon. It fell upon him the following year. Jerusalem was besieged and captured. Three thousand members of the nobility were taken captive to Babylon, and so were the temple treasures. Among the exiles was Ezekiel, who was both a prophet and a priest, and who foretold the departure of God's glory from the temple because of Judah's inveterate sin.

Nebuchadnezzar appointed Zedekiah to the throne of Judah, yet another of King Josiah's sons. He was a weak and indecisive character. His counsellors advised him to look to Egypt for help, but Jeremiah insisted that Judah's only hope of survival was to submit to Babylon. Himself a firm patriot, Jeremiah found it very hard to witness his country's humiliation, and even harder because of his policies to be suspected of treason. His was a voice crying in the wilderness. He stood and suffered alone.

Unfortunately, Zedekiah 'did not humble himself before Jeremiah the prophet, who spoke from the mouth of the Lord'.[96] In 589 B.C. he openly rebelled against Babylon. None of the hoped-for help from Egypt was forthcoming, and Jerusalem had to endure a second siege, this time for eighteen months. The famine conditions were appalling. Jeremiah continued to urge surrender, bringing upon himself first imprisonment and then an attempt on his life.

In 587/6 a breach was made in the walls and the city fell. The city walls were broken into rubble and Solomon's magnificent temple was burned to the ground.

The tiny remnant who were left were put in the charge of Gedaliah, and Jeremiah went on urging them to submit to the authority of Babylon. But Gedaliah was assassinated, and the survivors fled to Egypt, dragging the hapless Jeremiah with them.

The best way to feel Israel's despair when her temple had been destroyed and her people exiled is to read the Book of Lamentations:

'How lonely sits the city that was full of people!
How like a widow has she become, she that was great among the nations!
She that was a princess among the cities has become a vassal. . . .
From the daughter of Zion has departed all her majesty.
Her princes have become like harts that find no pasture;

they fled without strength before the pursuer. . . .
"Is it nothing to you, all you who pass by?
Look and see if there is any sorrow like my sorrow
which was brought upon me, which the Lord inflicted
on the day of His fierce anger." '[97]

Yet the godly were not taken by surprise. They knew
that God's covenant with Israel was founded not only on
His promise to be their God but on their undertaking to
obey. From the beginning Moses had warned them of the
consequence of disobedience, and the prophets had gone
on insisting that judgment was inevitable if the nation
did not repent:

'The Lord, the God of their fathers, sent persistently
to them by His messengers, because He had compassion
on His people and on His dwelling place'.[98]

The Restoration from Babylonian Captivity

The Babylonian captivity lasted about fifty years.
Although the exiles had been forcibly deported from their
homes, they seem to have enjoyed considerable freedom.
Jeremiah had written a letter to the first contingent of
exiles, telling them to 'build houses and live in them',
'plant gardens and eat their produce' and 'take wives
and have sons and daughters'.[99]

Their hardest trial was religious, for they felt spiritually
lost in their separation from temple and sacrifice. But
Ezekiel was among them to guide them. He still spoke to
them the word of the Lord. He even claimed to have seen
the glory of the Lord 'among the exiles by the river
Chebar'[100]—the very same glory which had dwelt in the
temple—so God could not after all have entirely abandoned them.

In the year 559 B.C. Cyrus II ascended the throne of
the nearby Persian kingdom. Nine years later, by over-

coming the Median army he became King of Media as well, and 'the Medes and Persians' (a familiar expression to readers of the Book of Daniel) became united. But this was only the beginning of Cyrus' brilliant military career. In 546 B.C. he defeated that byword of wealth, Croesus King of Lydia, and all Asia Minor was added to his empire.

The Jewish exiles must have heard of the exploits of Cyrus with growing expectation that their own deliverance from Babylon would not be long delayed. They knew that God was going one day to redeem them, for their prophets had always added visions of hope to their warnings of doom. In these promises of Yahweh the exiles put their trust.

The clearest and most immediate of such promises of salvation are to be found in Isaiah 40–55. There is a debate among Biblical scholars whether these chapters were really written 150 or 200 years previously by Isaiah or came from the pen of some anonymous contemporary prophet. If the authorship is in dispute, however, the message is not. Yahweh is not like the heathen idols. He is the living God, the creator of the world, and He rules in the kingdoms of men. Even heathen rulers are the instruments of His power. It is He who had raised up Cyrus to deliver His people:

'Who stirred up one from the east whom victory meets at every step?
He gives up nations before Him, so that He tramples kings under foot;
He makes them like dust with his sword, like driven stubble with his bow. . . .
Who has performed and done this, calling the generations from the beginning?
I, the Lord, the first, and with the last; I am He.'[101]

Thus says the Lord to His anointed, to Cyrus, whose

right hand I have grasped, to subdue nations before Him and ungird the loins of kings, to open doors before Him that gates may not be closed:

"I will go before you and level the mountains,
I will break in pieces the doors of bronze and cut asunder the bars of iron, . . .
For the sake of My servant Jacob, and Israel My chosen,
I call you by your name, I surname you, though you do not know Me.
I am the Lord, and there is no other, besides Me there is no God;
I gird you, though you do not know Me . . ." '[102]

In the year 539 B.C. the longed-for salvation was given. Belshazzar King of Babylon saw the handwriting on the wall, and that very night Babylon fell into the hands of the Persians. Immediately Cyrus issued two decrees, authorizing the Jewish exiles to return home and to rebuild their temple. The actual text of the second decree, including the materials and measurements of the temple to be built, has been preserved in Ezra 6.3–5. That Cyrus should have issued such an edict is fully consistent with his known policy. As Professor F. F. Bruce has written:

'Cyrus' conception of empire was widely different from Assyria's. The Assyrians imposed the worship of their chief gods on their subjects, and boasted in the subjugation of their subjects' gods. Cyrus . . . had no intention of offending his subjects' religious susceptibilities by such a policy; on the contrary, he would conciliate their susceptibilities by playing the part of a worshipper of their various gods.'[103]

It is hard to imagine the relief, the joy, the exultation of the Jewish exiles when the news of their deliverance reached them:

'When the Lord restored the fortunes of Zion, we were like those who dream. Then our mouth was filled with laughter, and our tongue with shouts of joy; then they said among the nations, "The Lord has done great things for them". The Lord has done great things for us; we are glad.'[104]

Indeed, as the Israelites reflected on their past history and on the steadfast love of their covenant God, they linked together three outstanding examples of His mercy. In each case He took the initiative in His sovereign grace, and in each case He called his people to the land of promise. In the first He brought Abraham from Mesopotamia, in the second the twelve tribes from Egypt, and in the third the exiles from Babylon.

Not that all the exiles took advantage of Cyrus' decree and accepted repatriation. A large number remained. The Book of Esther tells a dramatic story about some of them during the reign of Ahasuerus (Xerxes I), who ruled the Persian empire from 486–465 B.C.

The restoration took place in three clearly defined stages. Not all scholars agree about the order of events, but I give the traditional view. First, Zerubbabel left (538 B.C.) to restore the temple, then Ezra (458 B.C.) to restore the laws and lastly Nehemiah (445 B.C.) to restore the city wall.

The first and main party of Jews left Babylon for home in 538 B.C., a year or so after Cyrus' edict. They were led by Zerubbabel, grandson of King Jehoiachin, and Joshua the high priest. No sooner had they arrived in Jerusalem than they built the altar of burnt offering and laid the foundations of the temple. But then the Samaritans, on being refused the opportunity to collaborate, began to oppose the reconstruction. And the work ceased for about fifteen years.

That it restarted was due largely to the encouragement

of the prophets Haggai and Zechariah. Haggai reproved the people that they had built their own houses, while the Lord's house still lay in ruins:

'Who is left among you that saw this house in its former glory? How do you see it now? Is it not in your sight as nothing? Yet now take courage, O Zerubbabel, says the Lord; take courage, O Joshua, son of Jehozadak, the high priest; take courage, all you people of the land, says the Lord; work, for I am with you, says the Lord of hosts.'[105]

Zechariah added his word of exhortation:

'The hands of Zerubbabel have laid the foundation of this house; his hands shall also complete it.'[106]

So the work began again in the year 520 and was finished in 515, some seventy years after the destruction of its predecessor.

We now jump nearly seventy-five years in the story to the second stage in the reconstruction of Israel's national life after the exile. This was led by Ezra, who was a priest and a scribe, and (as several scholars have described him) a kind of 'Secretary of State for Jewish Affairs' in Babylonia. He was sent to Jerusalem by the Persian King Artaxerxes I (465–423 B.C.), with royal instructions 'to make enquiries about Judah and Jerusalem according to the law of your God'.[107] It was his task to regulate Israel's religious and moral responsibilities in accordance with the law.

Thirteen years later came Nehemiah, also sent by King Artaxerxes, with authority to rebuild the city, and in particular its walls. On arrival he lost no time, but said to the local officials:

'You see the trouble we are in, how Jerusalem lies in ruins with its gates burned. Come, let us build the wall of Jerusalem, that we may no longer suffer disgrace.'[108]

In spite of opposition and threats the task was accomplished in 52 days. Then a great public assembly was held, at which Ezra and the Levites read God's law aloud and expounded it to the people. There followed a public confession of national sin and a renewal of the covenant to keep God's law in the future. Finally the rebuilt wall was dedicated amid much rejoicing, 'and the joy of Jerusalem was heard afar off'.[109]

Unfortunately, as with previous national reformations, not all the undertakings of the people were kept. For when Nehemiah paid a second visit to Jerusalem a little later, he found several sad irregularities such as a failure to pay tithes, keep the sabbath and avoid intermarriage with the heathen. But Nehemiah dealt faithfully with these matters according to God's law.

It may well be that the prophecy of Malachi belongs to this period, for reference is made in it to identical or very similar malpractices—e.g. mixed marriage and divorce, laxity in the payment of tithes and the offering of blemished sacrifices to God.

The Inter-testamental Period

Israel had to wait another 400 years before her Messiah was born. This is called 'the inter-testamental period', since no book of either the Old or the New Testament was written during it. The voice of prophecy was known to be silent. The author of the First Book of the Maccabees, which belongs to the Apocrypha[110] and describes the events of 175–134 B.C., mentions this several times. He refers to a time of great affliction for Israel as being 'worse than any since the day when prophets ceased to appear among them'[111] and says that Simon was confirmed as leader and high priest in perpetuity 'until a true prophet should appear'.[112]

Nevertheless, there are references to this period in the

Book of Daniel, which is certainly one of the most difficult books in the Bible. Questions regarding its authorship, composition and interpretation continue to perplex scholars. It contains several remarkable dreams and visions, some of which are explained, while others are left wholly or partially without explanation.

In general, these predict the rise and fall of the great empires, especially as they affect the people of God. The best-known is Nebuchadnezzar's dream of a vast image or colossus, whose head was made of gold, breast and arms of silver, belly and thighs of bronze, legs of iron and feet of mixed iron and clay. Then (in the dream) a stone hit the feet, and the whole image was smashed to pieces. Daniel interpreted the dream as referring to successive empires. Traditionally, these have been understood as Babylon ('you, O King, . . . are the head of gold'), Medo-Persia (the breast and arms), Greece, the kingdom 'which shall rule over all the earth', and Rome, which became 'a divided kingdom' and did not stand. If this is right, then the stone, 'cut out by no human hand', is the kingdom of the Messiah, of which Daniel says:

'The God of heaven will set up a kingdom which shall never be destroyed . . . It shall stand for ever . . .'[113]

These great empires did follow one another. They provided the setting within which God's drama of redemption was acted out. The Babylonian kingdom lasted from 605 to 539 B.C., the Medo-Persian from 539 to 331, the Greek from 331 to 63, and the Roman from 63 on into the Christian era.

Later chapters of the Book of Daniel are more explicit. His vision recorded in chapter 8 is of a powerful ram, charging west, north and south, with no beast able to stand before it. Being two-horned, it represents the Medo-Persian empire (v. 20). Then 'a he-goat came from the west across the face of the whole earth.' This is 'the

103

King of Greece' (v. 21), that is to say, the rise of the Greek empire under Philip of Macedon. The he-goat from the west 'had a conspicuous horn' between its eyes, with which it struck the ram and broke its two horns. This prominent horn will be Philip's son, Alexander the Great, who, after a series of dashing victories against Asia Minor, Tyre, Gaza and Egypt, defeated the Persian army in 331 B.C.

'Then the he-goat magnified himself exceedingly' (v. 8), referring perhaps to the continuance of Alexander's campaign through Afghanistan as far as India. 'But when he was strong, the great horn was broken', for he died in 323 B.C. in Babylon, and 'instead of it there came up four conspicuous horns', for Alexander's empire was divided into four major regions under his generals— Macedonia and Greece, Thrace or West Asia, Syria and Babylonia (under Seleucus) and Egypt (under Ptolemy).

Of these the last two dominated the fortunes of Israel for the next 300 years. 'They brought untold miseries upon the world'.[114] As in earlier centuries Palestine was a buffer territory between the Assyrian-Babylonian-Persian empires to the north-east and the Egyptian to the south-west, so now Judea was caught between the Seleucids ruling Syria and the Ptolemies ruling Egypt. The former are termed 'the king of the north' in Daniel 11, and the latter 'the king of the south'. Both dynasties lasted until the middle of the first century B.C., and relations between them varied from uneasy co-existence to active hostility and warfare. Judea kept coming under the control now of the one, now of the other.

Returning to Daniel's vision of the he-goat, whose one conspicuous horn had been replaced by 'four conspicuous horns', the vision developed as follows:

'Out of one of them came forth a little horn, which grew exceedingly great toward the south, toward the east, and toward the glorious land. It grew great, even to the host of heaven . . . It magnified itself, even up to the Prince of the host; and the continual burnt offering was taken away from Him, and the place of His sanctuary was overthrown . . . and the truth was cast down to the ground . . .'.[115]

This 'little horn' is interpreted as 'a king of bold countenance' who 'shall cause fearful destruction . . . and shall destroy mighty men and the people of the saints'.[116] He seems without doubt to be Antiochus Epiphanes (175–163 B.C.), who is further designated 'a contemptible person' in Daniel 11.21.

In 167 B.C. Antiochus Epiphanes ordered the suspension of the temple sacrifices, the destruction of the Scriptures, and the discontinuance of circumcision, sabbath observance and the food laws. The climax came in December, when a new altar was dedicated to Zeus, 'the Lord of heaven' (of whom Antiochus claimed to be an incarnation), and unclean animals were offered upon it. Thus the continual burnt offering was taken away and the sanctuary profaned by 'the abomination that makes desolate'.[117]

The king's edict applied to the provinces as well as to Jerusalem, on pain of death. Many complied. Many others resisted, welcoming death rather than defilement. The most fearful tortures and massacres took place, some of which are described in the Books of the Maccabees. The martyrs died 'by sword and flame, by captivity and plunder'.[118] It is probably to them that the author of the Letter to the Hebrews was referring when he wrote:

'Some were tortured, refusing to accept release, that they might rise again to a better life. Others suffered mocking and scourging, and even chains and imprisonment. They were stoned, they were sawn in two,

105

they were killed with the sword . . . of whom the world was not worthy . . .'.[119]

Organized resistance was sparked off by the high priest Mattathias who took it upon himself to kill both a Jewish traitor and the king's officer who was inviting them to sacrifice. This led to a period of guerrilla warfare, in which pagan altars were demolished, Jewish children forcibly circumcised and compromisers slain.

Mattathias died in 166 and was succeeded in turn by three of his sons—Judas who was surnamed Maccabaeus, an epithet meaning probably 'the hammer' or 'the eradicator' (166–161 B.C.), Jonathan (161–143 B.C.) and Simon (143–135 B.C.). The details of their revolt against Gentile rule and of their extraordinary military exploits are recorded in the Books of the Maccabees.

Probably the most triumphant moment in their history came in 164 B.C. when, under the leadership of Judas Maccabaeus, the temple area was purified and the temple itself restored, a new altar was constructed and dedicated, and the sacrifices began to be offered again.

'On the anniversary of the day when the Gentiles had profaned it, on that very day, it was rededicated, with hymns of thanksgiving, to the music of harps and lutes and cymbals'.[120]

The war of independence continued for many years, and political autonomy was not secured until 128 B.C. under John Hyrcanus, Simon's son. He was priest and leader, and some said prophet and king as well. He and his sons annexed a good deal of the territory surrounding Judea.

But in 63 B.C. the Roman general Pompey entered Jerusalem, and penetrated even into the holy of holies, to the horror of the priests. Judea became a Roman protectorate, and Jewish independence was lost again.

In 40 B.C. Herod, who had already been military pre-fect of Galilee and later joint tetrarch of Judea, was made by the Roman senate 'King of the Jews'. Gradually he reconquered his kingdom and in the year 37 B.C. besieged and took Jerusalem, executing Antigonus, the last of the Maccabean priest-rulers. Herod was always unpopular as an Edomite foreigner (although a Jew by religion). Nevertheless he reigned for thirty-three years. It was under his aegis that in 19 B.C. the great reconstruction of the temple began. The work continued almost until A.D. 70, when the temple was again and finally destroyed, this time by the Roman army.

Throughout the uneasy period of Maccabean rule, important movements were taking shape in the Jewish community which later hardened into the various religious parties of our Lord's day.

The revolt of the Maccabees was first and foremost a religious protest, a defiant refusal to compromise with Hellenizing influences. Nothing aroused the indignation of the Maccabees more than the time-serving high-priests, installed by favour of the Seleucid kings. They and their followers are the 'renegade Jews' of the Books of the Maccabees, who wanted even to remove the marks of circumcision and so to ape Greek ways as to wear Greek dress and to build themselves a Greek stadium in which to compete in the games.

The Jews who avoided all contamination from Hellenizing influences were the *Hasidim* or pious ones. They were thoroughgoing separatists, the ancestors of the Pharisees, concerned for religious rather than political freedom.

The Hasmoneans (the Maccabees' family name) were not content with religious freedom; they wanted national independence too. They got involved in all kinds of political intrigue, and their successors were the Sadducees.

The political extremists, wanting to continue the

Maccabean struggle for independence, were the Zealots. They were revolutionary firebrands, determined at all costs to wrest their freedom from Rome.

When, in the fulness of time, Jesus Christ came, the people once tried 'to take Him by force to make Him king'.[121] But He withdrew from them. He had to explain that, although He was indeed a king, His kingdom was 'not of this world'.[122] The freedom He offered was freedom from the tyranny of sin.

> 'If you continue in My word, you are truly My disciples, and you will know the truth, and the truth will make you free'[123]

The Great Empires

(The dates B.C. are related to each empire's sovereignty as it affected Israel)

854–612	Assyrian
612–605	Egyptian
605–539	Babylonian
539–331	Persian
331–63	Greek (including Seleucids and Ptolemies)
63–	Roman

Some Dates to Remember

c. 1280	The Exodus from Egypt
c. 1050	The Monarchy established under King Saul
c. 1010	King David ascends the throne
c. 930	King Solomon dies. The divided monarchy begins—Israel lasting until 722 and Judah until 586
722	The Fall of Samaria and end of the Northern Kingdom
701	Jerusalem besieged by Sennacherib

For Further Reading

Israel and the Nations by F. F. Bruce (Paternoster 1963,
254 pages). An authoritative sketch of Israel's history
during the 1300 years from the Exodus to the fall of
the second temple in A.D. 70. The second half of the
book covers the inter-testamental period from the
accession of Alexander the Great (336 B.C.). The
illustrated edition (1969) includes 36 photographic
plates and 3 maps. The author is Rylands professor of
Biblical Criticism and Exegesis in the University of
Manchester.

A Christian's Guide to the Old Testament by John B.
Taylor (Hodder 1966, 94 pages). After marshalling four
basic reasons why Christians should read the Old
Testament, the Vice-Principal of Oak Hill College
describes an imaginary Hebrew family living in
Ramah 800 years before Christ, surveys Old Testament
history from Abraham to Nehemiah, and gives
admirable summaries of the Old Testament's thirty-
nine books and principal themes.

Archaeology of the Old Testament by R. K. Harrison (Hodder & Stoughton 1963, 162 pages). Although he describes it as 'an elementary introduction . . . for the unprofessional student', Professor Harrison (of Wycliffe College, Toronto) has written a thorough and well documented account of the more significant archaeological discoveries in Bible lands. His purpose is not so much to prove the truth of the Old Testament as to illumine the text by setting it in its 'true historical and cultural perspective'. Six chapters follow the chronology of the Old Testament from 'Mesopotamian Origins' to 'Exile and Restoration'; the final chapter is on the Dead Sea Scrolls. There are 2 maps and 12 photographic plates.

Old Testament Times by R. K. Harrison (IVP 1971, 357 pages). The author's basic conviction is that the Hebrew people cannot be understood in isolation from the whole Near Eastern history and culture to which they belonged. So he traces the history of the O.T. period from the patriarchs to the Maccabees in the light of modern archeological and sociological discoveries. An authoritative work, with over 100 photographic illustrations.

NOTES

1 Ps. 147.20

2 Gen. 1.1; Rev. 21.1, 5

3 The order in which the Old Testament books are placed is different in the Hebrew and the Christian Bibles. The Christian Church followed the arrangement in the Septuagint, the Greek translation made in the 2nd century B.C.

4 Although less familiar than 'Jehovah', this is probably the correct rendering of the Hebrew name YHWH, whose significance was revealed to Moses. See Exodus 3.13–15. It is usually translated

'the LORD' in English versions.

5 I recognize, however, that other Christians who accept and uphold the authority of Scripture reject the theory of evolution as being (in their view) incompatible with Biblical teaching. As the debate continues, it is particularly important for all of us (whichever position we hold) to try to distinguish both between scientific fact and scientific theory, and between what the Bible plainly asserts and what we may like to think it asserts. I have more to say on the whole question of Biblical interpretation in chapter 7.

6 Gen. 8.22

7 A temple-tower constructed of brick in the shape of a terraced pyramid and set on an artificial mound. Ziggurats are known to have been built in Babylonia as early as c. 3000 B.C.

8 Gen. 11.1–9

9 Gen. 12.1–3 RSV margin

10 Gen. 17.7

11 Gal. 3.29

12 Rev. 7.9; Gen. 22.17; Heb. 11.8–12, 16, 39, 40

13 e.g. to Abraham, Gen. 15.1–6; 17.1–8; 22.15–18; to Isaac, 26.1–5; to Jacob, 28.13–15 and 35.9–12

14 Gen. 23

15 Gen. 50.26

16 Ex. 1 11

17 Ex. 1.14

18 Ex. 12.40, 41

19 Ex. 2.24

20 Ex. 2.1–10

21 Ex. 2.11–15

22 Ex. 3.1–6

23 Ex. 3.15

24 Ex. 4.27–13, 16

25 Ex. 14.21

26 Ps. 106.8–10

27 Ps. 136.1, 2, 10–14

28 Ex. 19.4–6

29 e.g. Ex. 25.8 and 40.34

30 Lev. 16

31 Lev. 17.11

32 Lev. 16.21, 22

33 Ex. 40. 17

34 Num. 9.1–3

35 Num. 1.1 ff

36 Ex. 13.17 ff

37 Ex. 19.1 ff and Leviticus

38 Num. 10.11, 12

39 Num. 10.29

40 Num. 11.1–6

41 Num. 12

42 Num. 13.28, 29, 31

43 Num. 20.14 ff

44 Deut. 7.6; 10.12, 13

45 Deut. 11.26, 27; 30.15

46 Deut. 34.10
47 Josh. 1.6
48 Josh. 3.15, 16
49 Josh. 11.16, 17
50 Josh. 24.14, 15
51 Deut. 9.4, 5
52 Lev. 18.24–30
53 Judges 2.11–13
54 Judges 2.14
55 Judges 2.16
56 Judges 2.17
57 1 Sam. 3.20
58 1 Sam. 7.15–17
59 1 Sam. 8.1–3
60 1 Sam. 8.20
61 1 Sam. 15.23
62 2 Sam. 1.19
63 Ps. 51
64 2 Sam. 22.1–3, 32 and 33 = Ps. 18.1–3 and 31, 32
65 2 Sam. 7.11, 16
66 1 Kings 3.9
67 1 Kings 4.32–34
68 1 Kings 4.20, 25
69 1 Kings 11.1–8
70 1 Kings 12.4
71 1 Kings 12.7
72 1 Kings 12.28
73 1 Kings 18.21
74 1 Kings 18.36
75 1 Kings 21.19
76 2 Kings 14.25
77 Some, however, would date both Jonah and Joel earlier than Amos.
78 Am. 2.6–8
79 Am. 5.1–24
80 Hos. 6.6
81 Is. 7.4, 9
82 Am. 3.2
83 Mic. 6.6–8
84 Is. 1.8
85 2 Kings 18.32–34
86 2 Kings 19.6 cf. Is. 37.33–35
87 2 Kings 19.35 cf. Is, 37.36
88 Ps. 46.1, 10, 11
89 2 Chron. 34.3
90 2 Kings 23.25
91 Jer. 3.10
92 Jer. 7.24; 17.9; 31.33
93 Jer. 22.13–17
94 Jer. 36.21–23
95 Nahum 3.1, 5a–19b
96 2 Chron. 36.12
97 Lam. 1.1, 6, 12
98 2 Chron. 36.15
99 Jer. 29.5, 6
100 Ezek. 1.1
101 Is. 41.2, 4
102 Is. 45.1, 2, 4, 5
103 *Israel and the Nations* by F. F. Bruce (Paternoster 1963 Illustrated Edition 1969) p. 100
104 Ps. 126.1–3
105 Hag. 2.3, 4
106 Zech. 4.8
107 Ezra. 7.14
108 Neh. 2.17
109 Neh. 12.43
110 The 'Apocrypha' is an expression given to certain books which were not part of the Hebrew canon of the Old Testament. Some contain material which is evidently legendary, and others material which Christians read

for ethical rather than
doctrinal instruction.

111 1 Macc. 9.27
112 1 Macc. 14.41
113 Dan. 2.44
114 1 Macc. 1.9
115 Dan. 8.9–12
116 Dan. 8.23, 24
117 Dan. 11.31
118 Dan. 11.33
119 Heb. 11.35–38
120 1 Macc. 4.54
121 Jn. 6.15
122 Jn. 18.33–38
123 see Jn. 8.31–36

4. THE STORY OF THE BIBLE (NEW TESTAMENT)

In the previous chapter the story of the Old Testament has been sketched, covering several thousands of years. In this chapter an outline of the New Testament story will be given, covering less than a century. It is a fascinating tale of the words and deeds of Jesus of Nazareth, first of what He 'began to do and teach'[1] during His life on earth and then of what He continued to do and teach through His chosen apostles after He had returned to His Father and constituted His church.

The Four Gospels

Although there are a few scattered references to Jesus in contemporary secular writings, especially in Tacitus and Suetonius, the main source of our information about Him remains the four 'gospels'. They are rightly so called. For strictly speaking they are not biography, but testimony. They bear witness to Christ and to the good news of His salvation. Therefore their authors select, arrange and present their material according to their purpose as 'evangelists'. This gives us no ground to doubt their trustworthiness, however. On the contrary, we should approach the gospels with confidence, not suspicion. There are many reasons for doing so.

First, the four evangelists were certainly Christian men, and Christian men are honest men to whom truth matters.

Secondly, they give evidence of their impartiality by including incidents they would clearly have preferred to omit. For example, although by that time Peter was a highly respected church leader, neither his boastfulness nor his denial of Jesus is suppressed.

Thirdly, they claim either to be themselves eye-witnesses of Jesus or to report the experience of eye-witnesses. Although it seems likely that no gospel was actually published earlier than A.D. 60, we must not imagine that there was an empty gap between the ascension of Jesus and that date. This was the period of 'oral tradition', in which the words and deeds of Jesus were used in Christian worship, evangelism and the teaching of converts, and so began to be collected in writing. Luke says he drew on 'many' such compilations.[2]

Fourthly, Jesus seems to have taught like a Jewish Rabbi. He gave His instruction in forms (e.g. parables and epigrams) which a tenacious oriental memory would have had no difficulty in learning by heart, and in addition He promised that the Holy Spirit would stimulate the apostles' memory.[3]

Fifthly, if God said and did something absolutely unique and decisive through Jesus, as Christians believe, it is inconceivable that He would have allowed it to be lost in the mists of antiquity. If He intended future generations to benefit from it, He must have made provision for it to be reliably reported, in order to make the good news available to all men in all times and places. What He decided to do was to present the one gospel in four gospels.

As we read the gospels it becomes clear that they tell the same story, yet differently. The first three (Matthew, Mark and Luke) are usually known as the 'synoptic' gospels because their stories run parallel and present a 'synoptic' (i.e. similar) account of Jesus' life. Matthew and Luke appear to have known Mark's gospel and to have incorporated most of it in theirs. They also have some additional common material, generally known as 'Q' (the first letter of the German word *Quelle*, a source), though each has independent information as well. Scholars are not agreed how far the Synoptic Gospels were known or used by John, but most believe that his gospel was the last to be published.

The gospel of Mark is the shortest and probably the earliest of the four. The style is terse, the stories are vivid and the tone is exciting, with everything happening 'immediately' after something else. The apostle Peter referred to Mark as his 'son',[4] and the second-century fathers Papias and Irenaeus described him as Peter's interpreter. It may well be, therefore, that Peter's memoirs or preaching or both have been preserved in Mark's gospel, which has obvious similarities to Peter's *First Letter*.

It is possible that Matthew's name became attached to the first gospel because 'Q', consisting largely of the sayings of Jesus, was his collection. We know he was a tax-collector,[5] so that he will have been used to making notes and keeping records. Certainly, according to Papias, 'Matthew compiled the *logia*—sayings—in Hebrew (i.e. Aramaic, the language spoken by Jesus), and everybody translated them as he was able'.[6] His gospel is very Jewish and betrays his special interest in the fulfilment of prophecy.

116

Luke is the only Gentile among the New Testament authors. He had himself travelled widely and as one of Paul's companions will have absorbed the apostle's teaching about God's grace to the Gentiles. Consequently, he emphasizes the universal scope of Christ's love, as illustrated in his care for the despised 'outsiders' of contemporary Judaism—women and children, publicans and sinners, lepers, Samaritans and Gentiles.

John had evidently meditated long and deeply on the teaching of Jesus. His own thought and language became so completely assimilated to his Lord's that it is not always easy to tell when the one's words end and the other's begin. He leaves us in no doubt about the purpose of his gospel, for he himself defines it for us. He has, he says, recorded a number of the 'signs' which Jesus did, so that readers will believe in Him as the Christ, God's Son, and so receive eternal life.[7] True to his avowed purpose he assembles a variety both of signs and of witnesses, in order to demonstrate the unique 'glory' of Jesus.

The Birth and Youth of Jesus

Each evangelist begins his story at a different place. Mark plunges almost immediately into Jesus' public ministry, heralded as it was by John the Baptist. John goes to the other extreme and reaches back into a past eternity to the pre-incarnate existence of Jesus Christ. As 'the Word' He was with God in the very beginning. Indeed, He was Himself God, and was active in the creation of the universe. Long before He actually 'came' into the world by becoming flesh, He was continually 'coming into the world' as the true light (though unrecognized) to enlighten every man with the light of reason and of conscience.[8]

It is Matthew and Luke who tell us the actual story of

117

Jesus' birth. Luke tells it through the eyes of the Virgin Mary (perhaps even from her own lips), while Matthew tells it from Joseph's point of view.

Luke records the angel's announcement to Mary that both her conception and the boy to be born will be supernatural:

> 'And the angel said to her, "the Holy Spirit will come upon you, and the power of the Most High will overshadow you; therefore the child to be born will be called holy, the Son of God." '[9]

Luke goes on to describe how Mary shared her secret with her cousin Elizabeth who was shortly to give birth to John the Baptist; how Joseph (whose painful dilemma over Mary's pregnancy Matthew describes) travelled south with her from Nazareth to Bethlehem their ancestral home, in order to comply with the requirements of the imperial census; and how it was in the stable of a Bethlehem inn that Jesus was born and laid by His mother in a manger.

Although the world's Saviour was born in such lowliness, and received no public acclaim, there were those who came to pay homage to Him. Luke tells of certain shepherds who learned the good news from angels, and Matthew of mysterious Magi—astrologer-priests from Persia—who were guided to Him by a star. There seems to have been a deliberate providence in bringing these two contrasting groups. For the shepherds were Jewish, untutored and poor, while the Magi were Gentile, cultured and rich. Yet the barriers of race, education and social rank were transcended by their common worship of the infant Christ. They foreshadow the colourful diversity of Christ's followers.

Not everybody worshipped Him, however. Herod the Great, who in the course of his reign murdered every possible rival, was alarmed to hear the Magi say they had come to honour the King of the Jews. For he was the king of the Jews. So who was this? Warned by God of Herod's resolve to destroy the child, Joseph and Mary fled with Him to the safety of Egypt, and the one who was born to rule became a refugee.

Jesus was brought up in Nazareth in Galilee. His home must have been far from affluent, for when presenting their firstborn son to the Lord, Joseph and Mary brought a pair of pigeons as their offering, prescribed in the law for those who could not afford a lamb. But it will have been a happy home, shared (as the years passed) by the other children of the family. Joseph worked as a carpenter and taught his trade to Jesus, while Mary will have nurtured Him in godliness and righteousness by teaching Him to read the Scriptures and to pray. In the beautiful countryside around He will have become familiar with the lilies of the field and the birds of the air, to which He later referred, and with the living God who clothes and feeds them.

The only incident from Jesus' boyhood which is recorded in the gospels took place when He reached the age of twelve and was taken up to Jerusalem for the Passover, to prepare at thirteen to become a 'son of the commandment'. After the festival He was accidentally left behind. His parents found Him 'sitting among the teachers, listening to them and asking them questions'. These Jewish leaders were 'amazed at His understanding and His answers', and His parents were perplexed when He asked them: 'Did you not know that I must be in My Father's house?' His sense of communion with God as Father and of compulsion to do His will were to remain with Him throughout His later ministry.

Apart from this story, recorded in Luke 2:41–51, the verses which immediately precede and follow it tell us all we need to know about Jesus' youth. Both are bridge verses, verse 40 spanning the twelve years from His birth and verse 52 the remaining 18 or so years before His public ministry began. Both tell us that during these years Jesus was developing naturally yet perfectly, in body, mind and spirit. Here is verse 52:

'And Jesus increased in wisdom and in stature, and in favour with God and man.'

Although the evangelists are not concerned to give us a strictly chronological account of the Lord's public ministry, it appears from John's gospel to have lasted approximately three years.[10] We may call the first the year of obscurity, the second the year of popularity and the third the year of adversity.

The Year of Obscurity

All four gospels recount something of the ministry of John the Baptist. He was an ascetic, wearing nothing but a camel's hair cloak with a leather girdle, and eating an austerity diet of locusts and wild honey. Through his lips, after a silence of several centuries, the authentic voice of prophecy was again heard, as he summoned the people to repentance and to his baptism of repentance in preparation for the coming of the Messiah. Large crowds flocked to the River Jordan to listen to his preaching and to be baptized.

When Jesus presented Himself for baptism John demurred, for he had pronounced himself unworthy even to stoop down and undo the sandal strap of the one coming after him. But Jesus was resolved to fulfil all righteousness and, though He had no sins of His own to confess, to identify Himself with the sins of others. So He persuaded John to baptize Him. At that moment the Holy Spirit came upon Him like a dove, and the Father's voice was heard proclaiming Him in words of Old

Testament Scripture both His beloved son and His suffering servant.[11]

Immediately after His baptism, the same Spirit who had descended upon Him 'drove' Him into the Judean desert. Here He fasted for forty days in order no doubt to seek strength through prayer for the ministry to which He had just been commissioned. During this period He was also savagely tempted to compromise with the devil by trying to attain right ends by wrong means. But the Lord's hidden years of Scripture meditation stood Him in good stead. He was able to counter every diabolical suggestion with an apt Biblical rejoinder. For He was determined to live according to Scripture and so obey His Father's will.

It appears that after the temptation Jesus returned to the River Jordan and gave the two brothers Andrew and Simon Peter a kind of preliminary call to His service. They left John the Baptist and began to follow Jesus.

Returning north to Galilee, Jesus performed His first miracle, changing water into wine at a wedding in Cana. It symbolized His claim to introduce a new order, and by it He 'manifested His glory, and His disciples believed in Him'.[12]

Next He went up to Jerusalem for the Passover and boldly ejected from the temple courts the merchants and money-changers who had profaned it. When challenged about His action, He replied enigmatically:

'Destroy this temple, and in three days I will raise it up'[13]

It was another dramatic claim about the new order. For He was alluding not only to His physical body which would be raised from death in three days, but to His spiritual body, the church, which would live in the power of the resurrection. His church would also be a new and

121

spiritual temple, God's dwelling place, to replace Herod's material temple which would be destroyed.

One man who was deeply impressed by the early teaching and miracles of Jesus was a leading Jewish rabbi called Nicodemus. He came under cover of dark for a private interview, to be told by Jesus that the indispensable condition for seeing and entering God's kingdom was a new birth from above by the power of the Holy Spirit. Some time later on His way north again into Galilee, Jesus repeated this message or something very similar, though not now to a Jewish man, but to a Samaritan woman. She needed 'living water', He said, an inner 'spring of water welling up to eternal life', which would quench her thirst and which only He could supply.[14]

Other details of the first year of Jesus' ministry are not recorded. Most of it seems to have been spent in Judea. It was a transition period, during which His ministry overlapped with the ministry of His forerunner, John the Baptist. The disciples of Jesus were also baptizing. And gradually those following Jesus came to outnumber those following John, which John accepted with beautiful humility, saying:

'He must increase, but I must decrease.'[15]

But this situation was the signal for Jesus to leave Judea for Galilee. Soon afterwards John was arrested and imprisoned, and the Galilean ministry, the year of popularity, began.[16]

The Year of Popularity

Attending the synagogue service one sabbath day in His home town Nazareth, Jesus was given the scroll of Isaiah from which to read:

'The Spirit of the Lord is upon Me, because He has

anointed Me to preach good news to the poor. He has sent Me to proclaim release to the captives and recovering of sight to the blind, to set at liberty those who are oppressed, to proclaim the acceptable year of the Lord'.[17]

During the sermon which followed, Jesus dared to claim that He was Himself the fulfilment of this Scripture. At first the congregation were amazed at His gracious words. But when He went on to suggest that His ministry, like that of the prophets Elijah and Elisha, would be more acceptable to the Gentiles than to Israel, they were so infuriated that they drove Him out of the city and tried even to push Him over the nearby hill. It was a foretaste of His coming rejection, and forced Him to move His home and headquarters from Nazareth to Capernaum on the north-west shore of the lake.

From Capernaum during the rest of this second year Jesus made innumerable journeys throughout Galilee. Matthew sums up what form His ministry took:

'And He went about all Galilee, teaching in their synagogues and preaching the gospel of the kingdom and healing every disease and every infirmity among the people.'[18]

First, He preached. Mark says that the topic of His preaching was 'the gospel of God', summarized in these words:

'The time is fulfilled, and the kingdom of God is at hand; repent, and believe in the gospel.'[19]

This divine kingdom was the personal reign of God in the lives of men, and He (Jesus) had come to inaugurate it. Its arrival was in fulfilment of Old Testament expectation, and in order to 'receive', 'enter' or 'inherit' the kingdom men must repent and believe, humbly accepting

123

its privileges and submitting to its demands like little children.

Next, He taught. That is, He did more than announce the gospel of the kingdom and call men to enter it; He went on to teach His disciples the law of the kingdom. Of this we have no better summary than the 'Sermon on the Mount', consisting no doubt of instruction given over a protracted period. Its integrating theme is the call to His disciples to be different from both pagans and Pharisees. 'Do not be like them', He said. If they were to be the light of the world and the salt of the earth, their righteousness must exceed that of the scribes and Pharisees. They must not try (like the casuists) to dodge the law's demands, or (like the hypocrites) to practise their piety before men, but realize that God sees in secret and looks on the heart. His disciples must be quite different from the Gentiles as well, in their love, their prayers and their ambition. They must love their enemies as well as their friends, renounce vain repetitions in prayer for an intelligent approach to their Father, and seek first, as the supreme good, not their own material necessities but the rule and the righteousness of God.

The people were astounded by Jesus' authority, for He taught neither like the scribes (who invariably quoted their authorities), nor even like the prophets (who spoke in the name of Jehovah), but with His own authority and in His own name, declaring 'truly, truly, I say to you'.

Moreover, He enforced His teaching with unforgettable parables, which illustrated the love of God for sinners (e.g. the Prodigal Son), the necessity of humble trust in God's mercy for salvation (e.g. the Pharisee and the Publican), the love which we ought to have for each other (e.g. the Good Samaritan), the way God's word is received and God's kingdom grows (e.g. the Sower and the Mustard Seed), the responsibility of disciples to develop and exercise their gifts (the Pounds and the

Talents), and the judgment of those who reject the gospel (e.g. the Wheat and the Tares).

Thirdly, He healed. He performed other miracles too, exhibiting His power over nature by stilling a storm on the lake, walking on water and multiplying loaves and fishes. But His commonest miracles were healing miracles, effected now by a touch of the hand, now by a bare word of command. From one point of view, the sufficient explanation of His healing ministry is His love, for He was moved to compassion by the sight of every form of suffering. But, in addition, His miracles were 'signs' both of God's kingdom and of His own deity. They signified that the Messiah's reign had begun, as the Scriptures had foretold. It was with this evidence that Jesus sought to reassure the doubts of John the Baptist in prison:

'Go and tell John what you have seen and heard: the blind receive their sight, the lame walk, lepers are cleansed, and the deaf hear, the dead are raised up, the poor have good news preached to them.'[20]

Similarly, the miracles were signs that the forces of evil were in full retreat before the advancing kingdom of God:

'But if it is by the finger of God that I cast out demons, then the kingdom of God has come upon you.'[21]

The miracles were also signs that Jesus was the Son of God, for each was an acted parable, dramatizing one of His divine claims. The feeding of the 5,000 set forth visibly His claim to be the bread of life, His healing of the man born blind His claim to be the light of the world, and His raising of the dead His claim to be the resurrection and the life.

In this threefold work of preaching, teaching and healing, Jesus also involved the Twelve. He seems to have chosen and called them early in this second year of His public ministry and, by surnaming them 'apostles', to have indicated the work to which they were being commissioned. I shall enlarge on this in a later chapter when we consider their unique authority. In human terms they were a motley and unpromising group, including four fishermen, one tax collector, at least one political zealot and another who proved to be a traitor. Yet He kept them with Him, training them by what they saw and heard, and sent them out two by two, endowed with His authority to preach and to heal like Him.

During the Galilean ministry the crowds kept growing. The whole countryside became tense with excitement and expectation:

'Great multitudes gathered to hear and to be healed of their infirmities.'[22]

The high tide of Jesus' popularity seems to have been reached at the time of the feeding of the 5,000. It took place just after the beheading of John the Baptist, an ugly omen of the turn of the tide. Since the 5,000 were all men, apart from women and children,[23] the total crowd must have been more than double that number. When the hunger of all had been satisfied as a result of the miraculous multiplication of five barley loaves and two pickled fish, the buzz of excitement reached fever pitch. The word began to go round the crowd 'This is surely the prophet who is to come into the world'. And as the rumour spread, the people made up their minds. They were determined to 'take Him by force to make Him king', that is, their national leader to liberate them from the dominion of Rome. But Jesus caught wind of it, and 'withdrew to the hills by Himself'.[24]

The Year of Adversity

Having returned to Capernaum on the other side of the lake, Jesus preached a sermon in the synagogue, using the miracle of the loaves and fishes as His text. He had not come to be a political revolutionary. He was the bread of life, He said. Anyone who came to Him and believed in Him would never again be hungry or thirsty. And the bread He would give for the life of the world was His flesh. Immediately a dispute broke out among the Jews:

'How can this man give us His flesh to eat?'

Even His disciples found it a hard saying, and many of them 'drew back and no longer went about with him'.[25] The tide had turned.

So now Jesus again 'withdrew' and made more distant expeditions, beyond the boundaries of Galilee. He went to Tyre and Sidon in the north-west,[26] and to the Decapolis, a region south-east of the Lake.[27] Then later He travelled north again, this time to Caesarea Philippi, in the foothills of Mount Hermon.[28] Here a very important incident took place, which forms a kind of watershed in the gospel narrative. Jesus asked the Twelve who men were saying He was, and they gave Him the answers of popular speculation, that He was John the Baptist, Elijah or one of the prophets. But who did the Twelve say He was? Immediately Peter replied, 'You are the Christ'.

Our Lord's rejoinder comes as a shock to many readers, for He commanded them to tell no one about Him.[29] But the next verse explains the riddle:

'And He began to teach them that the Son of man must suffer many things, and be rejected by the elders and the chief priests and the scribes, and be killed, and after three days rise again. And He said this plainly.'[30]

Jesus' command to silence, repeated after several of the miracles, was due to His desire to keep His Messiahship secret so long as the people misunderstood its nature, as exemplified in their attempt to make Him a king by force.

But now that Peter had clearly confessed his faith, Jesus 'began' to teach the necessity of His sufferings and to do so 'plainly', i.e. openly. At first Peter could not accept this truth. But Jesus insisted on it and added that the same pattern of glory through suffering or life through death would be the experience of His followers as well.[31]

Six days later according to the synoptic evangelists Jesus took Peter, James and John with Him up a 'high mountain' (? Hermon) and was transfigured before them, His face and clothing becoming suffused with a bright light. It was a preview of His glory, the glory of His kingdom and of His resurrection body, the glory to which He would one day come through suffering.

When Jesus returned to Galilee it was for a largely private visit, since He was continuing to teach the disciples about His coming sufferings, and subsequent resurrection.[32] Soon after He began His journey south.[33] Indeed, 'He set His face to go to Jerusalem,[34] and on the way continued to emphasize the same things.[35] Luke supplies a number of details about this journey and its accompanying instruction, which the other evangelists do not record.[36] He tells us that Jesus referred to a baptism of suffering which He had to undergo and to His sense of constriction until it was accomplished.[37] Later He said:

'Behold, we are going up to Jerusalem, and everything that is written of the Son of man by the prophets will be accomplished'.[38]

The approach to Jerusalem was through Jericho, an oasis not far from where the Jordan flows into the Dead Sea. Here Jesus gave sight to blind Bartimaeus and salvation to Zacchaeus the shady tax-collector.[39] Then came the steep ascent along the desert road towards the holy city.

The impression conveyed by the Synoptic evangelists

is that Jesus went straight to Jerusalem and to the events of His last week. We know from John's gospel, however, that He spent about another six months in Judea, which included visits to Jerusalem for the Feast of Tabernacles in October and the Feast of Dedication in December.[40] Exactly where He was staying during this period is not clear, but sometimes it was in the wilderness of Judea and sometimes even the other side of the Jordan near the scene of His baptism.[41]

When He appeared in public for the festivals, His claims (attested by His signs) became ever clearer and bolder. He was the bestower of living water, He said, the light of the world (as evidenced in giving sight to a man born blind), the great 'I am' who lived eternally before Abraham, the good Shepherd who would lay down His life for His sheep and (when He raised Lazarus from death) both the resurrection and the life.[42] The Jewish leaders found these claims increasingly provocative, and it is several times recorded that they tried to arrest and kill Him.[43]

Already during His Galilean ministry, although the crowds gave Him tumultuous support, He did not escape the carping criticisms of the scribes and Pharisees. Mark assembles a series of four 'controversy stories' in which Jesus was accused first of blasphemy (for daring to forgive a man's sins), then of fraternizing with sinners, thirdly of religious laxity in failing to fast, and lastly of breaking the sabbath.[44] In defending Himself against these charges Jesus had only made matters worse in His critics' eyes by claiming to be the Son of man with authority to forgive, the physician who had come to heal sick sinners, the bridegroom in whose presence the wedding guests could not fast and the lord even of the sabbath.

As time passed He had gone further. He had condemned the Pharisees for their hypocrisy[45] and for exalting their man-made traditions above God's commandments,[46] and was later to rebuke the Sadducees for their ignorance of God's word and God's power.[47] Gradually the tension grew. The Jewish leaders were jealous of His reputation with the people, wounded by His exposure of their superficiality and put to shame by His own transparent integrity. It was only a matter of time before the final collision.

When Jesus approached Jerusalem for the last time and reached the point on the road round the Mount of Olives where the city came into view, He could not restrain His tears. He wept and said:

'Would that even today you knew the things that make for peace! But now they are hid from your eyes.'[48]

Nevertheless, despite what it seemed would be the city's certain rejection, He issued one last appeal. By a careful pre-arrangement He was able to ride into Jerusalem on a borrowed donkey, in order deliberately to fulfil the prophecy of Zechariah:

'Rejoice greatly, O daughter of Zion! Shout aloud, O daughter of Jerusalem! Lo, your king comes to you; triumphant and victorious is He, humble and riding on an ass, on a colt the foal of an ass.'[49]

The crowds that were accompanying Him were eager to acclaim Him. They cut branches from the trees and took off their cloaks to make a carpet for Him to ride over. They waved palm branches in the air and shouted their Hosannas. For this was His 'triumphal entry' into Jerusalem. But His triumph was not shared by the authorities, and it was short-lived. He antagonized them by cleansing the temple for the second time,[50] and during the next three days, from Monday to Wednesday, their hostility to Him became increasingly intense. They engaged Him in controversy, theological and political, although they could not fault Him in argument.[51] He

for His part castigated the Pharisees for their religious
pretence in a series of devastating 'woes',[52] and warned
His apostles of the coming destruction of Jerusalem and
of the opposition they must expect before His return
would bring history to its end.[53]

The Death and Resurrection of Jesus

The Thursday of this last week was by one reckoning the
eve of the Passover and by another the Passover itself.
Jesus knew that His 'hour', which He had repeatedly said
was 'not yet', had at last come. It was to be an hour of
unparalleled suffering, and yet also the hour of His
'glorification' by which He would be most fully revealed
and the salvation even of the Gentiles would be accomplished.[54]

He spent His final hours of liberty privately with the
Twelve in a furnished, first-floor room lent Him by a
friend. Here they ate the Passover meal together. During
supper He performed a slave's work, which evidently
none of them had been willing to do, for He went round
washing their feet. He told them that they must humble
themselves and love one another like that. During and
after supper He also gave them bread and wine as emblems
of His body and blood which were to be offered for their
salvation, and commanded them to eat and drink in His
memory. Then He fortified them by profound instruction
about the new and intimate relationship with Him which
the coming Holy Spirit would make possible, and He
prayed for them that the Father would keep them what
they were, a distinct people, who no longer belonged to
the world but were to continue living in it as His representatives.

It must have been late when they left the upper room,
walked through the deserted city streets, crossed the
Kidron valley and began to climb the Mount of Olives.

In the garden of Gethsemane Jesus prayed with an agony of desire that He might be spared having to drink 'this cup', an Old Testament symbol of God's wrath upon sin. But he ended each prayer with a fresh surrender of His will, and emerged with a quiet, unshakeable resolve to drink it. At that very moment the temple soldiers arrived to arrest Him, carrying torches and weapons, and Judas betrayed Him to them.

There now followed a gruelling series (that night and the following morning) of six separate trials, three in Jewish courts, one before Herod and two before Pontius Pilate. When false witnesses accused Him, Jesus was silent, but when the high priest challenged Him whether He was 'the Christ, the Son of God', He boldly acknowledged that He was and was immediately condemned to death for blasphemy. This travesty of justice was made the more bitter for Him by the brutality of those who struck Him and spat in His face, and by the cowardly denials of Peter in the courtyard outside.

Since by Roman law the Jews were not permitted to carry out the death sentence, it was necessary for them to get it ratified by the procurator. Pontius Pilate is known to have been an efficient administrator, but ruthless. He quickly saw through the political charge of which the Jews accused Jesus, namely that He had forbidden the payment of tribute to Caesar and had made claims to be a king Himself. A few questions about Jesus' kingship satisfied him that the prisoner was no revolutionary agitator. But Pilate was a man ruled more by expediency than by principle. He wanted both to release Jesus and to satisfy the Jews simultaneously. So he tried various compromise arrangements. Would they be content if Jesus received a scourging, or a trial by Herod or the customary Passover clemency? But the Jews would not allow him to escape a decision. When they hinted that if Pilate released Jesus he would forfeit Caesar's favour, his mind was made up. He washed his hands publicly in feigned innocence and handed Jesus over to them to be mocked, flogged and crucified.

Crucifixion was a horrible form of execution. To the Romans it was a shameful thing; they reserved it for slaves and the worst criminals. It was a sadistic kind of torture too, for it deliberately prolonged the pain and postponed death sometimes even for days.

How Jesus viewed and endured His ordeal is shown by the seven 'words' which He spoke from the cross. The first three indicate that He was able so to forget His own suffering as to concern Himself entirely with the welfare of others. He prayed that His tormentors might be forgiven; He commended His mother to John's care, and John to His mother's; and He assured the penitent brigand who was being crucified at His side that He would be with Him that very day in paradise.[55] After this Jesus seems to have been silent for several hours, while a strange darkness overshadowed the land. Then he uttered four cries, perhaps in quick succession, which give us some idea of the nature and purpose of His sufferings.[56] First, 'I thirst', betraying His physical anguish. Then 'My God, My God, why hast thou forsaken Me?' This cry of dereliction was framed as a question not because He did not know the answer, but because He was quoting Psalm 22.1. And He quoted it (as He always quoted Scripture) because He believed He was fulfilling it. The Godforsakenness which He experienced was the divine judgment which our sins deserved. He was drinking the 'cup' of God's wrath. Almost immediately came a loud cry of triumph, the single word 'Finished', expressing His accomplishment of the sin-bearing work He had come to do. Finally, He commended His spirit to the Father, to show that His death was a voluntary, self-determined act:

133

'Father, into Thy hands I commit My spirit'[57]

About thirty-six hours later God raised Him from the dead, as a decisive proof that He had not died in vain. At first light of dawn on Easter Day, Mary Magdalene and some other women came to Joseph of Arimathea's tomb, in order to complete the burial rites which the onset of the sabbath had interrupted. But they found that the stone had been rolled aside from the mouth of the tomb and that the tomb itself was empty. Hearing the news, Peter and John raced to the sepulchre. Looking in, they discovered not only that the Lord's body had gone, but that His grave-clothes were still there, lying in an undisturbed condition. It was clear circumstantial evidence that the body had not been touched by human hands but raised from death by God. They 'saw and believed'.

Then the risen Lord began to appear. First individually to Mary Magdalene and to Peter. Then to two disciples on the road from Jerusalem to Emmaus. Then to the apostles the same evening, and again the following Sunday when Thomas (absent the previous week) was with them. Next, when they had returned to Galilee, He appeared to them there also, both on a mountain and on the lakeshore. At every appearance He gave them evidence that it was He Himself, the same person as before His death, though now marvellously changed, and He commissioned them to go into the whole world and to make all nations His disciples.

These appearances continued for forty days. The last one took place on the Mount of Olives. Having promised them power to be His witnesses once the Holy Spirit had come upon them, and having blessed them, He was 'taken up . . . into heaven'. There is no need to doubt the literal nature of His ascension, so long as we realize its purpose. It was not necessary as a mode of departure, for 'going to the Father' did not involve a journey in space and presumably He could simply have vanished as on previous occasions. The reason He ascended before their eyes was rather to show them that this departure was final. He had now gone for good, or at least until His coming in glory. So they returned to Jerusalem with great joy and waited—not for Jesus to make another resurrection appearance, but for the Holy Spirit to come in power, as had been promised.

The Infant Church

The disciples had only ten days to wait. Then suddenly, while they were praying together for the promise to be fulfilled, it happened. Accompanied by the noise of wind and the appearance of fiery flames, the Holy Spirit came and filled them all. It was the culminating event of Christ's saving career, for, as Peter explained in his sermon that same morning, it was Jesus Christ who brought the significance of His birth, death, resurrection and ascension to its climax by pouring out His Spirit from heaven.

Pentecost must also be understood as a fundamentally missionary event. The miracle of the foreign languages which the disciples spoke symbolized the international Christian community which was about to be brought to birth by the gospel.

Three thousand people were converted, baptized and added to the church that day:

'And they devoted themselves to the apostles' teaching and fellowship, to the breaking of bread and the prayers'[58]

One marvels at the clarity and forcefulness of the early preaching of the apostles. Luke gives us four sample sermons by Peter—on the Day of Pentecost, after the healing of the cripple outside the temple's Beautiful

Gate, before the Jewish Council and to the household of Cornelius.[59] Although of course he supplies only a précis of each, it is enough to show the content and pattern of Peter's proclamation.

Peter preached Jesus Christ, His life, death and resurrection. During His life He was divinely attested by miracles. His death was due both to the purpose of God and to the wickedness of men.[60] Though men denied and killed Him, God vindicated Him by raising Him from the dead. And now He is exalted as Lord, Christ, Saviour and Judge. Moreover, all this is doubly confirmed by the testimony of Old Testament Scripture and of the apostolic eye-witnesses. Therefore, let them repent of their sin, believe in the name of Jesus Christ and be baptized, for then they will receive the blessing promised to Abraham's seed, namely the forgiveness of sins and the gift of the Spirit.

It must not be imagined, however, that the infant church had no problems. No sooner had Jesus Christ through His spirit launched His offensive to conquer the world than the devil mounted a powerful counter-attack. His strategy was threefold.

First, he tried the crude weapon of persecution.[61] When Peter and John started 'teaching the people and proclaiming in Jesus the resurrection of the dead',[62] they were arrested and brought to trial before the Sanhedrin. Here they witnessed to Jesus with wonderful boldness, declaring Him to be the only Saviour. The council was deeply impressed, knowing them to be uneducated men, but forbade them to 'speak or teach at all in the name of Jesus'. Peter and John replied that they must obey God not men, and that in any case they simply could not help speaking of what they had seen and heard. Then, after they had been further threatened, they were let go. The apostles went straight to their Christian friends and together they prayed to the sovereign Lord of nature

and of history not for their safety and protection, but that they might be given courage to go on speaking His word. So the preaching went on. They were again arrested, and now imprisoned, but an angel of the Lord released them and told them to go and preach the gospel in the sacred precincts of the temple itself. Once more they were arrested and brought to trial, but this time the Jewish Council, cautioned by the Pharisee Gamaliel that they might be found opposing God, did no more than beat them and repeat their injunction not to speak in the name of Jesus. The reaction of the apostles?

'They left the presence of the council, rejoicing that they were counted worthy to suffer dishonour for the name. And every day in the temple and at home they did not cease teaching and preaching Jesus as the Christ'[63]

The other weapons which the devil wielded against the church were more subtle. Unable to crush it by external pressure, he tried to undermine it from within.

The generosity of the early Christians had led many of them to sell their lands and bring the proceeds to the apostles for the relief of those in need. A married couple called Ananias and Sapphira decided to do the same, but then to keep back part of the money for themselves while pretending to surrender it all. Their property was entirely at their own disposal both before and after the sale, as Peter later made clear. They were under no obligation to give any of it away. Their sin was that they wanted the credit for giving everything, without the cost. If they had succeeded in their intrigue, hypocrisy would have begun to seep into the Christian community. Peter detected their lie, however, and they paid for their duplicity with their lives.[64]

The third Satanic weapon was the most indirect. It was to preoccupy the apostles with social administration (to be precise, the care of Christian widows) and so divert them from the teaching role to which God had called them. But the apostles were alert to this danger. So they delegated the task. They instructed the body of the disciples to choose seven 'deacons' (as they are usually called) to take over the church's welfare work, so that they could devote themselves to their God-given priority, namely 'to prayer and to the ministry of the word'.[65]

When the devil's initial three-pronged counter-offensive had failed, Luke was able to write:

'And the word of God increased; and the number of the disciples multiplied greatly in Jerusalem.'[66]

One of the seven was Stephen, a Christian man full of grace, faith, wisdom and power. Accused of speaking against the law of Moses and the temple, he was brought before the Council. His defence, recorded in Acts 7, is a masterly narrative of God's dealings with Israel, designed to demonstrate that God is tied to no place or building but only to His people whose God He is. He

138

ended his speech by accusing his accusers. They were stiff-necked, he said, always resistant to the Holy Spirit, and now guilty of murdering the Christ. At this they rushed on him, threw him out of the city and stoned him to death.

But in the providence of God the death of the first Christian martyr helped rather than hindered the spread of the gospel. For the persecution of Christians which followed it scattered them throughout Judea and Samaria, and wherever they went they preached the word.[67] Among them was Philip, who was another of the seven 'deacons'. He was given conspicuous success in evangelizing Samaritans, who for centuries had been repudiated by the Jews. So the apostles (who had stayed behind in Jerusalem) sent Peter and John to investigate and endorse what had happened, thus avoiding a continuance within the church of the Jewish-Samaritan schism. Philip also explained the good news of Christ crucified to an Ethiopian state official who was on his way back home from Jerusalem.[68]

This outreach to Samaria and Ethiopia was only the prelude to the Gentile mission which soon began. Luke introduces it in *Acts* with two significant conversions, of Saul of Tarsus and (through Peter's witness) of the Roman centurion Cornelius. These events indicate the vital part played by the great apostles Paul and Peter in opening the gates of the church to Gentiles.

Saul of Tarsus is first mentioned as the man who minded the clothing of those who were stoning Stephen. It is conjectured that he never forgot the courage and love of this Christian martyr who prayed for the forgiveness of his enemies. But he continued to stifle the voice of conscience and savagely to persecute the church, until that memorable day (described no fewer than three times in *Acts*) when Jesus Christ appeared to him on the road to Damascus and (as he was later to put it) 'apprehended' him. After reaching Damascus he learned from Ananias that he had been called to be an apostle as well as a disciple, and to be Christ's chosen instrument to carry His name before Gentiles as well as Jews.[69] His conversion must have taken place between three and five years only after the crucifixion.

Almost two complete chapters of *Acts* are devoted to the story of Cornelius' conversion, so important an event did Luke consider it.[70] For Cornelius, although a 'godfearer' on the fringe of the synagogue, was still a Gentile outsider. It took a special vision to convince Peter that he should enter Cornelius' house and preach the gospel to him, and it took a special repetition of Pentecost (as I think we may describe it) to convince him that God now made no distinction between Jews and Gentiles but granted His cleansing and His Spirit to all believers without discrimination.[71] It was an immense leap forward.

Some of those who left Jerusalem after Stephen's martyrdom travelled north to Antioch, which was the capital of Syria and the third most renowned city in the Empire. They preached the Lord Jesus to the Greeks, and a great number believed. Hearing about this, the Jerusalem church sent Barnabas to Antioch, and he in his turn fetched Paul to help him. For a whole year these two men taught the converts. Here (in Antioch) the first Gentile church was established, for the first time the disciples were called Christians, and the first missionary expedition was launched.[72] The date was now about 47 A.D.

The First Missionary Journey

The missionaries chosen, set apart by the church in obedience to the Spirit's leading, were Barnabas and Paul, who then invited Mark (Barnabas' cousin) to accompany them. They sailed to Cyprus, Barnabas' home country, and then north-west to land on Asian soil at Perga in Pamphylia. By this time Mark had had enough and returned to Jerusalem. Perhaps he was scared of the swamps of Pamphylia where (conjecturally) Paul caught malaria which damaged his eyesight. At all events, when they had climbed the plateau and reached Galatia, Paul seems to have had some disfiguring eye disease.[73] The first Galatian city he visited was Pisidian Antioch, where he preached in the synagogue and many Jews were converted. But when the unbelieving Jews contradicted Paul's message, he took a bold step (which in the future he would often repeat) and turned to the Gentiles. Driven out of the city by opposition, Paul and Barnabas moved on to three more Galatian towns, Iconium, Lystra (where pagans nearly worshipped them as gods and Jews stoned Paul as a blasphemer) and Derbe. Then, retracing their steps, they strengthened the new converts and in every church appointed elders to care for them.[74]

Back in Antioch they gathered the church together and reported what God had done, especially 'how He had opened a door of faith to the Gentiles'.[75] But the church's rejoicing soon gave place to controversy, for there arrived in Antioch from Jerusalem a group of so-called 'Judaizers', who started teaching that unless Gentile converts were circumcised and kept the law of Moses they could not be saved.[76] Paul engaged them in a vigorous debate. And when even Peter, in a temporary lapse due to fear rather than conviction, withdrew from fellowship with Gentile Christians, Paul had to rebuke him publicly.[77]

It appears that the insidious influence of the Judaizers had penetrated even to the Galatian churches. This prompted Paul to write the first of his many letters. In his *Letter to the Galatians* he defended his apostolic authority as derived from Christ, assured them that there

141

was no discord between him and the Jerusalem apostles, rejected the Judaizers' gospel as being no gospel at all, emphasized that salvation is by God's grace alone through faith alone without the addition of circumcision or the works of the law or anything else, and begged his Galatian readers to stand fast in their Christian liberty.

The church of Antioch decided to send Paul and Barnabas to Jerusalem to settle the issue which had been raised by the Judaizers, and this led to 'the Council of Jerusalem' (described in Acts 15) in about 49 or 50 A.D. After much debate Peter (who by now had recovered from his lapse) recounted the conversion of Cornelius. Then Paul and Barnabas told what God had done through their ministry among the Gentiles. Finally James, the Lord's brother, clinched the argument from Old Testament Scripture. Gentile converts, he concluded, did not need to be circumcised in order to be saved. Nevertheless, in order to respect the scruples of weak Jewish consciences and so promote Gentile-Jewish fellowship within the church, they were to be asked voluntarily to follow certain Jewish food and marriage regulations.[78]

It is almost certainly to this James that we owe the New Testament *Letter of James*. It may have been written about this time. It is evidently a Jewish Christian homily, whose emphasis is that a true, living and saving faith will be evidenced by a life of brotherly love, self-control and devotion to God.

The Second Missionary Journey

Armed with a letter from the Jerusalem apostles and elders, containing the decisions of the Council, Paul set out on his second missionary journey, this time accompanied by Silas.[79] They revisited the Galatian churches, delivering the Council's decree. At Lystra Paul invited Timothy to accompany them. Because he had a Gentile

142

father, Paul even circumcized him out of deference to local Jews, for now that the principle of salvation by grace alone had been established he was ready to make such a policy concession.[80]

Forbidden by the Holy Spirit (in ways not explained) to journey either south-west towards Ephesus or due north into Bithynia, Paul and his companions were shut up to going in a north-westerly direction and so arrived at Troas on the Aegean coast. Here Paul had a dream in which a Greek begged him to go over to Macedonia and help them. He and his friends interpreted the vision as a call from God to take the gospel into Europe. And Luke, the author of *Acts*, by using the pronoun 'we' for the first time in his narrative, quietly indicates that he sailed with them.

Macedonia was the northern province of Greece, and the missionary team preached the gospel in three of its principal towns—Philippi (where Paul and Silas spent a memorable night in prison, with their feet in the stocks), Thessalonica (where during a three-week mission a great many believed) and Beroea. Paul then moved on to Achaia, the southern province of Greece, visiting its two chief cities, Athens and Corinth.

There is something very moving about the picture of Paul in Athens, the Christian apostle alone amid the glories of ancient Greece. As he walked through the city it was not the beauty which struck him, however, but the idolatry. This stirred him deeply, and first in the synagogue with the Jews, then in the market place with passers-by, and finally before the famous Council of the Areopagus with the Stoic and Epicurean philosophers, he faithfully preached Jesus, the resurrection and the judgment to come.

Timothy joined him while he was in Athens, but Paul was so concerned to discover how the Thessalonian church was faring under persecution that he sent him off again at once to find out and to encourage them to stand firm.[81] By the time Timothy returned, Paul had moved on to Corinth.[82] The good news he brought was the occasion of his *First Letter to the Thessalonians*, with *the Second Letter* following it soon afterwards. In these letters Paul rejoices over the Thessalonians' faith, love and steadfastness, and over the example which they are setting to all the believers in Macedonia and Achaia.[83] He goes on to defend his personal integrity against his Jewish detractors.[84] Then he exhorts his readers to earn their own living and not to give up work on the false supposition that the Lord's return is imminent; to take courage in their bereavement because the living will not take precedence over the dead when Jesus comes; and to live lives of sexual purity. Perhaps he has these three categories in his mind when he writes:

'Admonish the idle, encourage the fainthearted, help the weak.'[85]

Paul stayed in Corinth for the best part of two years. He followed his normal custom of bearing witness to the Jews first, and won a notable convert in Crispus, the ruler of the synagogue. But when the Jews opposed and abused him, he again turned to the Gentiles and received support in his policy from an unexpected quarter, the proconsul of Achaia called Gallio. It was a truly wonderful triumph of God's grace that a Jewish-Gentile church should arise in such a cesspool of vice as Corinth was.

The Third Missionary Journey

Paul's voyage back to Antioch was interrupted by a brief visit to Ephesus, the principal city of the Roman province of Asia. He must have been so impressed by its strategic importance, that he went almost straight there at the beginning of his third missionary journey.[86] After three months' preaching in the synagogue he broke fresh ground in evangelistic method. He hired 'the hall of Tyrannus', presumably a secular school or lecture hall, and here every day for two years, according to some manuscripts 'from the fifth hour to the tenth' (i.e. from 11 a.m. to 4 p.m.), argued the gospel. Assuming that he worked a six-day week, this represents 3,120 hours of gospel argument. It is not surprising that as a result 'all the residents of Asia heard the word of the Lord'.[87]

While he was in Ephesus, the Corinthian church gave him much cause for anxiety on both doctrinal and moral grounds. His first letter to them (mentioned in 1 Cor. 5.9) has been lost. However, on receiving disquieting news from some Corinthian travellers, who also brought with them a number of questions from the church, Paul wrote them a second letter which is our *First Corinthians*. In it he is able to thank God for the gifts with which Christ has enriched them,[88] but he deplores the factions into which the church has been split and their false view of the ministry which lies behind the factions.[89] He also expresses indignant horror at the immorality and litigation which they are tolerating among their members,[90] and at the irregularities they are permitting in public worship.[91] In answer to their questions he writes about marriage,[92] about the eating of food offered to idols,[93] and about the use and abuse of spiritual gifts.[94] He then summarizes his gospel and emphasizes particularly the resurrection of Christ and of Christians.[95]

This letter evidently failed to have its desired effect, for Paul decided to visit Corinth personally. He later referred to this as a 'painful visit',[96] because apparently one of the church leaders openly defied his authority. So serious was this challenge that on leaving Paul wrote them yet another letter (usually referred to as the 'severe letter'), insisting that the offender be punished. This letter also seems to have been lost, unless (as some scholars

145

believe) it has somehow found its way into 2 Corinthians 10–13. At all events, the severe letter was heeded and the offender was duly disciplined. Paul was overjoyed to hear from Titus of their loyalty[97] and immediately wrote to them again.

In this letter, our *Second Corinthians*, he begs them now to 'forgive and comfort' the rebel, who has received a sufficient punishment.[98] He goes on to write of the glory, problems and responsibilities of the Christian ministry,[99] devotes two chapters to the appeal that he has launched to the churches of Macedonia and Achaia to raise money for the impoverished church of Judea,[100] and concludes with a lengthy defence of his apostolic authority.[101]

He mentioned in this letter his intention to pay them a third visit,[102] which eventually came to pass. Ephesus boasted a magnificent temple to the goddess Artemis (or Diana), which was one of the seven wonders of the world. As the number of Ephesian converts from idolatry grew, the silversmiths saw a strong threat to their trade in shrines or souvenirs of the goddess.[103] A serious riot ensued, and Paul left the city for Macedonia and then Achaia.[104]

It appears that the apostle stayed about three months in Corinth in the home of Gaius, and that from here he wrote his great *Letter to the Romans*.[105] In it he tells the Christians in Rome how eager he is not only to visit and encourage them, but also to preach the gospel in the world's capital city[106] and then to travel on into Spain.[107] So he takes the opportunity to unfold at length this gospel which is committed to him and to which he is committed. He describes the terrible degradation of mankind, and argues that there is no distinction between Jew and Gentile in the fact of their sin and guilt.[108] Neither is there any distinction between them regarding the offer of salvation:

146

'For there is no distinction between Jew and Greek; the same Lord is Lord of all and bestows His riches upon all who call upon Him.'[109]

This salvation is a free gift offered by God's grace, grounded upon Christ's death and—as the Old Testament itself makes plain—received by man's faith not earned by his works.[110] Faith not only justifies the sinner, but unites him to Christ. And 'in Christ', that is, joined to Christ by faith (invisibly) and by baptism (visibly), the Christian begins an altogether new life of freedom. He is free from the dominion of sin through slavery to God,[111] free from the bondage of the law through the indwelling Spirit,[112] and free from all fear of evil, whether in life or in death, through the assurance of being God's son for ever.[113]

Next Paul wrestles with a problem which troubled him deeply: How is it that the Jews, God's specially privileged people, have not accepted Jesus as their Messiah? It is certainly not that God's word of promise has failed. The strange phenomenon of their unbelief can be understood in the light partly of the mysterious process of God's election,[114] partly of their own rebellion as 'a disobedient and contrary people',[115] and partly of a broad historical perspective that one day 'the fulness' of Jews as well as Gentiles will come in and 'so all Israel will be saved'.[116]

After this digression Paul comes back to the life of practical holiness which, because of 'the mercies of God', all His people should lead—in mutual service,[117] in conscientious citizenship,[118] and in the brotherly love which accepts even the weak brother who has an over-scrupulous conscience.[119]

Leaving Corinth, Paul and his companions began their long journey to Jerusalem,[120] taking with them the now completed collection for the Judean church. Among the ports at which they called were Troas (where Paul's sermon lasted till midnight and their fellowship till daybreak!) and Miletus (where Paul gave a moving address to the elders of the Ephesian church).

Paul's Arrest and Journey to Rome

When at last they reached their destination, they had not been in Jerusalem a week before some Asian Jews started maliciously alleging that Paul had undermined Moses' law by his teaching and defiled the temple by bringing Greeks into it. A riot broke out, and Paul was rescued from being lynched by the prompt action of the military tribune.[121]

During the next two years and more the apostle was held a prisoner. During the same period Luke was at liberty in Palestine, no doubt gathering material for his Gospel and the *Acts*. Paul had to undergo a series of trials in Jerusalem and Caesarea before the Sanhedrin,[122] before the procurator Felix,[123] before his successor Festus,[124] and before King Agrippa and his wife Bernice.[125] But since as a Roman citizen he had exercised his right to appeal to Caesar, he was eventually sent to Rome for trial.

The long and perilous sea voyage included the exciting escape from shipwreck on the island of Malta, which Luke tells with graphic detail,[126] and at last Paul reached the Rome of his dreams. The Christians welcomed him, and the Jews came to visit him and hear the gospel from his lips.

Luke has now traced the spread of the gospel from Jerusalem the capital of Jewry to Rome the capital of the world. He ends his narrative with a picture of his hero, the apostle Paul, who although under house arrest was still an indefatigable evangelist:

'he . . . welcomed all who came to him, preaching the

148

kingdom of God and teaching about the Lord Jesus Christ quite openly and unhindered.'[127]

It was not only by spoken witness, however, that the apostle exploited his two years' imprisonment in Rome. He also spent time writing to various churches, and the so-called 'prison epistles' which belong to this period are the letters to the *Ephesians* (probably a circular letter to Asian churches of that region), to the *Colossians*, to *Philemon* (a personal letter instructing him to receive back as a brother his runaway slave, now converted) and to the *Philippians* (though some think this letter was written earlier from a supposed imprisonment in Ephesus). It is not easy to give a resumé of the message of these letters, for each was occasioned by a different local situation. Yet if there is one truth which stands out in them all, it is the greatness of Jesus Christ. The very fulness of God, Paul writes, was pleased both to dwell in Him and to work through Him, on the one hand creating the universe and on the other reconciling all things to Himself. He has now been exalted to God's right hand, far above all principalities and powers, and has been given the pre-eminent name, so that every knee should bow to Him and every tongue confess Him Lord. This cosmic Christ is also the head of the church, whose members are called to be what they are, a holy, united and victorious people.

The supremacy of Christ is also the theme of a very different New Testament book, the *Letter to the Hebrews*. Both its author and its destination are unknown, for neither is named in it. But its purpose is to prevent certain Jewish Christians from lapsing into Judaism, by emphasizing the finality of Jesus Christ. In Him all priesthood and sacrifice have been fulfilled, and by Him an eternal redemption has been won.

Since Luke concludes the *Acts* with Paul's arrival and ministry in Rome, we are left somewhat in the dark about the following years. But it seems certain that Paul was released from custody (as he expected) and that he resumed his travels for another year or two. He visited Crete and left Titus there.[128] Soon afterwards he wrote him his *Letter to Titus* to remind him of his responsibilities. He must appoint suitable elders in every town who would be able to combat false teaching. He himself should also be a teacher and emphasize the kind of Christian conduct which is appropriate in those who have embraced 'the sound doctrine' of the gospel of salvation.

Paul then went on to Ephesus, where he left Timothy for similar reasons.[129] In his *First Letter to Timothy* he gives him instructions how to deal with false teachers, conduct public worship, select candidates for the pastorate, exercise his own ministry in such a way that his comparative youth will not be despised, arrange for the care of Christian widows, give balanced advice about money and behave like a man of God. It is a truly 'pastoral epistle' (as the letters to Timothy and Titus are usually known), containing much practical wisdom for church leaders today.

Then Paul journeyed on, perhaps to Colosse,[130] then to Macedonia[131] and then across Greece to Nicopolis,[132] the capital of Epirus on the Adriatic. Perhaps it was his intention when winter ended to sail from there for Spain. Whether he succeeded we may never know, though early tradition says he did. In any case, at some point he was re-arrested. It may have been at Troas, so that he had to leave his personal possessions behind, including a cloak and some books and parchments.[133] This time his prison in Rome was not the comparative liberty of a house arrest, but probably a dismal underground dungeon.

From such an imprisonment he wrote his *Second Letter to Timothy*. He felt keenly his loneliness, for only Luke was with him. He begged Timothy to come and visit him soon, and in any case before the winter would make sailing impossible. But his great concern was not for himself but for the gospel, the precious 'deposit' which he had committed to Timothy and which Timothy must now hand on to faithful men who would pass it to others also. Timothy must persevere in it himself and guard it from every falsification. He must be prepared, if need be, to suffer for it. Above all, he must preach it urgently and faithfully. Paul himself had preached the gospel fully during the first hearing of his case, so that 'all the Gentiles', crowded into the place of his trial, had heard it.[134] It was a fitting conclusion to his life of testimony. Now at last he could say:

'I have fought the good fight, I have finished the race, I have kept the faith. Henceforth there is laid up for me the crown of righteousness, which the Lord, the righteous judge, will award to me on that Day. . . .'[135]

Tradition says that Paul was beheaded (as a Roman citizen would have been) on the Ostian Way. His execution was probably a part of the persecution which broke out in Rome in A.D. 64 when Nero tried to deflect responsibility for the great fire from himself to the Christians.

This same Neronian persecution forms the background to the *First Letter of Peter*. He wrote it from Rome[136] and addressed it to Christians in the northern parts of Asia Minor to whom, he anticipated, the persecution was about to spread. He calls it a 'fiery ordeal'.[137] They are not to be surprised by it as something strange, nor to be afraid, but rather to rejoice at their privilege of sharing Christ's sufferings.[138] Indeed, the patient endurance of undeserved suffering is an inescapable part of the Christian calling, since Christians are followers of Christ,

151

the suffering servant of the Lord.[139] The apostle Peter had soon to put his own instruction into practice, for he too (like Paul) was executed during the Neronian persecution, according to tradition by being crucified upside down.

The New Testament ends as *The Acts* begins, namely with Satanic attacks on the church from within and from without. The three *Letters of John*, written some time after the martyrdoms of Paul and Peter, warn the churches of the neighbourhood of Ephesus of a particular kind of Gnosticism. The heretics concerned denied that Jesus was 'the Christ come in the flesh', claimed to enjoy an experience of God without having to be righteous, and made arrogant pretensions to a superior enlightenment which led them to despise the unenlightened. Over against them John emphasized the truth of the divine-human person of Christ, the necessity of moral obedience and the centrality of love. The *Second Letter of Peter* and *the Letter of Jude* were also written to counter the promoters of 'anti-nomianism', false teachers who degraded Christian liberty into licence.[140] God's judgment would fall upon them.

The background to *the Book of Revelation* is probably the more severe and widespread persecution which was initiated by the Emperor Domitian (A.D. 81–96). Because of his faithful testimony John finds himself exiled to the little island of Patmos, some miles off shore from Ephesus.[141] Here he is given an 'apocalypse' or unveiling. In a sense the books of *Acts* and of *Revelation* are complementary. For *Acts* portrays the beginning of the church's mission and persecution as they appeared on the stage of history, whereas *Revelation* enables us to peep behind the scenes and glimpse the unseen spiritual battle which is raging between Christ and Satan.

John's visions are full of weird symbolism. Satan appears as 'a great red dragon with seven heads and ten horns', who declares war on the church. His three allies are two fearful monsters and a gaudy prostitute. The 'beast rising out of the sea' represents the persecuting power of the state, the second 'beast which rose out of the earth' (also called 'the false prophet') represents the cult of emperor-worship and indeed all erroneous teaching, while 'the great harlot' clothed in scarlet and decked with jewels, whose name is 'Babylon', represents the sinful enticements of worldliness. Persecution, error and evil are still the three major weapons which the devil wields in his fight against the church. But he will not prevail against it.

For *the Book of Revelation* is supremely a revelation of Jesus Christ as the Lamb who fights and conquers the Dragon. He is seen in other guises too, now patrolling and supervising His church, now sharing the Father's throne, now riding forth on a white horse as King of kings and Lord of lords to judge the nations, now coming as the Bridegroom to claim His bride. The whole book is a *sursum corda*, summoning hard-pressed Christian people to lift up their hearts and take courage. For Christ Jesus has died to ransom His people for God out of every nation. He is reigning now from His heavenly throne. And He is coming soon to judge and to save.

The church's prayer, with which the Bible ends, is 'Come, Lord Jesus.' And the church's assurance throughout its tribulation is that, until He comes, 'the grace of the Lord Jesus Christ' is sufficient to sustain all His people.[142]

Some Dates to Remember

The chronology of the New Testament period is difficult to determine with precision, although some dates are known. In areas of uncertainty, however, scholars differ from one another only by a year or two. One of the more commonly accepted reconstructions of events is given below.

B.C.

c. 5   The birth of Jesus

4   The death of Herod the Great

A.D.

30   The death, resurrection and ascension of Jesus. Pentecost.

c. 33   The conversion of Saul of Tarsus

44   The death of Herod Agrippa I (Acts 12.20–23)

c. 47, 48 The first missionary journey (Acts 13, 14)

c. 49   The Council of Jerusalem (Acts 15)

c. 49–52 The second missionary journey (Acts 16.1–18.22)

c. 52–56 The third missionary journey (Acts 18.23–21.17)

c. 57   Paul's arrest in Jerusalem (Acts 21.27–23.30)

c. 57–59 Paul's imprisonment in Caesarea (Acts 23.31–26.32)

c. 60, 61 Paul under house arrest in Rome (Acts 28.14–31)

c. 62–64 Paul at liberty again

64   The fire of Rome. Nero's persecution of Christians

c. 65   The martyrdom of Paul

70   The destruction of Jerusalem by Titus

81–96 The reign of the emperor Domitian. Widespread persecution

c. 100   The death of the apostle John

For Further Reading

A Christian's Guide to the New Testament by Alan Cole (Hodder and Stoughton 1965, 96 pages). Simple, introductory chapters on the earliest Christian preaching, the first Christian letters, the gospels (Christian 'newscasts'), the Acts, Christian prophecy (especially the Revelation), and forming and using the Christian library. Written in a racy style by a scholar with missionary experience in Asia.

The Life and Teaching of Jesus Christ by James S. Stewart (The Church of Scotland Committee on Youth. 1933. Second edition 1957, 209 pages). Written as part of the Church of Scotland's four years' course for Bible classes, this book by a distinguished theologian-preacher is both instructive and readable. After introductory chapters on 'The Gospel Records' and 'The Fulness of the Time' the story of Christ's life is unfolded stage by stage, and is interspersed with summaries of His teaching on particular subjects.

Archaeology of the New Testament by R. K. Harrison (English Universities Press 1964. 138 pages). Written as a companion volume to *Archaeology of the Old Testament*, and as one of the 'Teach Yourself' books, Professor Harrison summarizes the major discoveries which throw light on the content of the Gospels, the Acts and the Epistles. There are useful chapters on both the Nag Hammadi papyri and the Dead Sea scrolls and their relation to the New Testament, and nine photographic plates.

New Testament Times by Merrill C. Tenney (IVF 1965, 396 pages). A well-documented standard work of reference by the former Dean of the Graduate School, Wheaton College, Illinois. The historical, political, cultural and religious background is first thoroughly portrayed. The author then takes us systematically through the New Testament, making judicious and enlightening comments on the way. Copiously enriched by photographs, maps and charts. A mine of information.

NOTES

1 Acts 1.1
2 Lk. 1.1–4
3 Jn. 14.25, 26
4 1 Pet. 5.13 cf. Acts 12.11, 12
5 Mt. 9.9
6 Eusebius' *Ecclesiastical History* III.39.16
7 Jn. 20.30, 31
8 Jn. 1.1–14
9 Lk. 1.35
10 John mentions three Passovers in his narrative (2.13; 6.4 and 11.55)
11 Mt. 3 cf. Ps. 2.7 and Is. 42.1
12 Jn. 2.1–11
13 Jn. 2.19
14 The story of Nicodemus is recorded in Jn. 3.1 ff. and of the woman of Samaria in Jn. 4.4 ff.
15 Jn. 3.22–30
16 Jn. 3.24; 4.1–3; Mk. 1.14
17 Lk. 4.18, 19
18 Mt. 4.23 cf. 9.35
19 Mk. 1.14, 15
20 Lk. 7.22
21 Lk. 11.20
22 Lk. 5.15
23 Mt. 14.21
24 Jn. 6.14, 15
25 Jn. 6.52, 66
26 Mk. 7.24
27 Mk. 7.31
28 Mk. 8.27
29 Mk. 8.30
30 Mk. 8.31, 32
31 Mk. 8.34–38
32 Mk. 9.30, 31
33 Mk. 10.1
34 Lk. 9.51
35 e.g. Mk. 10.32–34, 45
36 see Lk. 9.51–18.14
37 Lk. 12.50
38 Lk. 18.31
39 Lk. 18.35–19.10
40 Jn. 7.2, 10, 14; 10.22, 23
41 Jn. 10.40; 11.54
42 Jn. 7.37–39; 8.12 and 9.5; 8.58; 10.11; 11.25, 26
43 Jn. 5.18; 7.30, 32; 8.59; 10.39; 11.53, 57
44 Mk. 2.1–3.6
45 e.g. Lk. 11.37–52
46 Mk. 7.1–13
47 Mk. 12.18–27
48 Lk. 19.41, 42
49 Zech. 9.9; Mt. 21.5
50 Mk. 11.15–19
51 Mk. 12
52 Mt. 23
53 Mt. 24; Mk. 13; Lk. 21
54 Jn. 12.20–33
55 Lk. 23.34; Jn. 19.26, 27; Lk. 23.43
56 Jn. 19.28; Mk. 15.33, 34; Jn. 19.30; Lk. 23.46
57 Lk. 23.46
58 Acts 2.42
59 Acts 2.14–40; 3.12–26; 5.29–32; 10.34–43

60 Acts 2.23
61 Acts 3–5
62 Acts 4.1, 2
63 Acts 5.41, 42
64 Acts 5.1–11
65 Acts 6.1–6
66 Acts 5.7
67 Acts 8.1–4
68 Acts 8.5–40
69 Acts 9.15
70 Acts 10, 11
71 Acts 10.47; 11.17; 15.7–11
72 Acts 11.19–26; 13.1–3
73 Gal. 4.13–15
74 The story of the first missionary journey is told in Acts 13.4 to 14.28
75 Acts 14.27
76 Acts 15.1, 5
77 Gal. 2.11–14
78 The Greek word translated 'unchastity' in Acts 15.20, 29 (RSV) may refer to fornication in particular, or to immorality in general, or (it has been argued) to Jewish regulations regarding marriage within the prohibited degrees.
79 The story of the second missionary journey is told in Acts 15.36–18.22
80 Acts 16.1–4; cf. 1 Cor. 9.19, 20
81 1 Thess. 3.1–5
82 1 Thess. 3.6; Acts 18.5
83 1 Thess. 1
84 1 Thess. 2
85 1 Thess. 5.14
86 The story of the third missionary journey is told in Acts 18.23–21.16
87 Acts 19.8–10
88 1 Cor. 1.4–9
89 1 Cor. 1.10–4.21
90 1 Cor. 5, 6
91 1 Cor. 11
92 1 Cor. 7
93 1 Cor. 8–10
94 1 Cor. 12–14
95 1 Cor. 15
96 2 Cor. 2.1
97 2 Cor. 1.12–14
98 2 Cor. 2.5–11
99 2 Cor. 3–6
100 2 Cor. 8, 9
101 2 Cor. 10–13
102 2 Cor. 12.14; 13.1
103 Acts 19.23–41
104 Acts 19.21, 22; 20.1, 2
105 Rom. 16.23; 1 Cor. 1.14
106 Rom. 1.8–15
107 Rom. 15.18–29
108 Rom. 1–3.20
109 Rom. 1.16; 3.22, 23; 10.12, 13 and also chapters 9–11
110 Rom. 3.21–5.21
111 Rom. 6
112 Rom. 7.1–8.13
113 Rom. 8.14–39
114 Rom. 9
115 Rom. 10. See especially verse 21
116 Rom. 11, especially verses 12, 25 and 26
117 Rom. 12
118 Rom. 13

119 Rom. 14, 15
120 Acts 20.3–21.16
121 Acts 21.17–22.29
122 Acts 22.30–23.10
123 Acts 24.1–21
124 Acts 25.1–12
125 Acts 25.13–26.32
126 Acts 27.1–28.10
127 Acts 28.30, 31
128 Tit. 1.5
129 1 Tim. 1.3
130 Philem. 22
131 1 Tim. 1.3
132 Tit. 3.12
133 2 Tim. 4.13
134 2 Tim. 4.17
135 2 Tim. 4.7, 8
136 cf. 1 Pet. 5.13 where 'Babylon' is almost certainly a symbol for Rome
137 1 Pet. 4.12
138 1 Pet. 4.13
139 1 Pet. 2.18–25
140 cf. 2 Pet. 2.19
141 Rev. 1.9
142 Rev. 22.20, 21

5. THE MESSAGE OF THE BIBLE

It is a fundamental Christian conviction that God has spoken, and spoken in a concrete historical and geographical setting. We have taken several chapters to survey the geography and the history; it is time now to listen to the message. Some of this has already been included in the story of the Bible, as the teaching of the prophets has been fitted into the life of Israel and the teaching of Christ and His apostles into the New Testament story. We saw also in the first chapter that the message of the Bible concerns salvation through Christ. But this needs to be elaborated.

Since the Bible is a whole library of books, composed by many human authors over more than a thousand years, it seems to some quite incredible that we can claim for it a single theme, let alone condense it into a single chapter. Besides, they say, do not the Old and New Testaments contradict each other? Does not the Old Testament portray Jehovah as a fearful God of wrath and judgment, who is entirely incompatible with the God and Father of our Lord Jesus Christ? How can we reconcile the thunders of Sinai with the meekness and gentleness of Christ?

159

I hope that the true answer to these questions will become plain as in this chapter I try to demonstrate further the astonishing unity of the Bible. Meanwhile, it will be enough to express the Bible's own claim that it contains neither a ragbag of miscellaneous contradictions, nor a gradual evolution of human ideas about God, as men grew up and discarded their childish notions, but a progressive revelation of truth by God.

Progression there undoubtedly is. For example, the great stress of the Old Testament is on the unity of God, in contrast to the degraded polytheism of the heathen nations. Although there are adumbrations of the Trinity in the Old Testament, this doctrine is clearly stated only in the New Testament. Again, there is progression from the recorded teaching of Jesus to the fuller understanding of His person and work which we find in the Epistles and the Prologue to the Fourth Gospel. But this is exactly what Jesus Himself led us to expect by what He said to the apostles in the upper room:

'I have yet many things to say to you, but you cannot bear them now. When the Spirit of truth comes, He will guide you into all the truth; for He will not speak on His own authority, but whatever He hears He will speak, and He will declare to you the things that are to come. He will glorify Me, for He will take what is Mine and declare it to you. All that the Father has is Mine; therefore I said that He will take what is Mine and declare it to you.'[1]

Progression is not the same as contradiction, however. An artist begins by making a sketch, and then applies his oils to the canvas bit by bit until the whole picture (present to his mind from the start, though not to the beholder's) finally emerges. Again, parents teach their children step by step, 'precept upon precept, precept upon precept, line upon line, line upon line, here a little, there

160

a little'.[2] But if they are wise, they do not teach anything in the early stages which needs later to be contradicted. Their later teaching supplements what has gone before and builds on it; it does not come into collision with it. So God has gradually filled out His revelation, constantly expanding it but never repudiating it, until at last it was complete in Christ the Word made flesh (than whom a higher revelation is inconceivable) and in the witness of the apostles to Christ.

The Letter to the Hebrews opens with a very valuable statement of this truth:

'In many and various ways God spoke of old to our fathers by the prophets; but in these last days He has spoken to us by a Son . . .'[3]

Here the author concedes that there are several differences between the Old and New Testament revelations. The revelation was given at different times ('of old' and 'in these last days'), to different people ('to our fathers' and 'to us') and especially in different modes ('in many and various ways . . . by the prophets' and 'by a Son'). But though the occasion, the recipients and the manner of the revelation were different, its author was the same. It is *God* who spoke to the fathers in various ways through the prophets, and it is *God* who has spoken to us in and through His Son.

In the light of this we should not hesitate to claim God Himself as the ultimate author of both Testaments or to designate the whole of Scripture 'the Word of God'. I shall have more to say in the next chapter about this.

What, then, has God spoken? The Bible is essentially a revelation of God. It is, in fact, a divine self-disclosure. In the Bible we hear God speaking about God. To say this is not inconsistent with the thesis developed in the first chapter that the Bible is concerned with salvation and bears witness to Christ. For what God says about

Himself is, above all else, that He has conceived and fulfilled a plan to save fallen men through Christ.

The Living and Consistent God

But before we come to His saving activity, there are two basic truths about Him to consider, which Scripture emphasizes throughout. The first is that He is a living and sovereign God; the second that He is consistent, always the same, 'the Father of lights with whom there is no variation or shadow due to change'.[4]

Again and again the one, living and true God is contrasted with the dead idols of heathendom. Prophets and psalmists hold heathen idols up to ridicule. Isaiah describes the scene in one of the temples when Babylon was captured. He pictures the chief Babylonian deities being snatched ignominiously from their pedestals, carried out on men's shoulders and loaded on to carts outside. Fancy gods being carried by men and becoming 'burdens on weary beasts'! And when the laughter subsides, the voice of God is heard. He is no idol needing to be carried about by men, for it is He who carries His people:

'Hearken to Me, O house of Jacob,
all the remnant of the house of Israel,
who have been borne by Me from your birth, carried from the womb; even to your old age I am He, and to grey hairs I will carry you. I have made, and I will bear; I will carry and will save.'[5]

Not only the idols' inability to save aroused the prophets' scorn, but their total lifelessness:

'Their idols are silver and gold, the work of men's hands.
They have mouths, but do not speak; eyes, but do not see.

162

They have ears, but do not hear; noses, but do not smell.
They have hands, but do not feel; feet, but do not walk; and they do not make a sound in their throat.'[6]

In contrast to them, 'our God is in the heavens; He does whatever He pleases'.[7] He is the living God, who sees and hears and speaks and acts.

This living God is sovereign, a great king over all the earth. He is king of nature, and king of the nations also.

As king of nature He sustains the universe He has made and all its creatures. Even the ferocious elements are under His control. 'The sea is His, for He made it',[8] and the 'stormy wind' fulfils His command.[9] Psalm 29 gives a dramatic description of a thunderstorm, in which 'the voice of the Lord' breaks the cedars of Lebanon. The lightning flashes. The wilderness is shaken. The forests are stripped bare. The rain causes floods. As havoc spreads, one would expect apprehension and alarm to spread with it. But the psalmist remains quietly confident that God is in control:

'The Lord sits enthroned over the flood; the Lord sits enthroned as king for ever'.[10]

Psalm 104 is a primitive study in ecology. In it the psalmist marvels[11] at the way storks make their homes in firtrees, while 'the high mountains are for the wild goats' and 'the rocks are a refuge for the badgers' (i.e. the rock hyrax). The psalm goes on to describe how God feeds all animals:

'These all look to Thee, to give them their food in due season.
When thou givest to them, they gather it up;
when Thou openest Thy hand, they are filled with good things.'[12]

163

Entirely in keeping with this Old Testament insistence that God is the Lord of nature is the teaching of Jesus in the sermon on the mount, that God rules the animate and inanimate worlds. On the one hand He feeds the birds of the air and clothes the lilies of the field; on the other 'He makes His sun rise on the evil and on the good, and sends rain on the just and on the unjust'.[13]

The king of nature is also king of nations. As Daniel said to King Nebuchadnezzar, 'the Most High rules the kingdom of men and gives it to whom He will'.[14] We saw in an earlier chapter how the little countries of Israel and Judah often seemed no more than pawns on an international chessboard. The great power blocks of the day were the empires of Egypt and Mesopotamia. As they confronted each other on the battlefield, and the tide of war ebbed and flowed, it was Israel and Judah and the small neighbouring states which got caught in between. Yet Israel continually uttered the splendid shout of faith:

'The Lord reigns; let the peoples tremble!'[15]

No power on earth, whether alone or in coalition with others, could triumph over God's people without God's permission. Do the nations scheme and plot, and set themselves against the Lord and against His anointed?

'He who sits in the heavens laughs; the Lord has them in derision.'[16]

The apostles of Jesus in New Testament days had the same conviction. When Peter and John were forbidden to speak or teach at all in the name of Jesus, they called their friends to prayer. They lifted their voices together to God as the 'sovereign Lord', the creator of the universe. Then they recited the first two verses of Psalm 2 (from which I have just quoted) and applied them to

164

Herod and Pontius Pilate, the Gentiles and the rulers of Israel. These had conspired together in Jerusalem against Jesus. To do what? 'To do whatever Thy hand and Thy plan had predestined to take place.'[17]

More than that. The prophets taught that the mighty soldier-emperors of the day, some of whom were cruel and ruthless men, were yet instruments in the hand of the Lord. Shalmaneser of Assyria was the rod of His anger, the staff of His fury, with which to punish Samaria,[18] Nebuchadnezzar of Babylon His 'servant' through whom He would destroy Jerusalem[19] and Cyrus of Persia His 'anointed' to free His people from their captivity.[20]

If the God of the Bible is the living and the sovereign God, He is also always self-consistent. His sovereign power is never arbitrarily used. On the contrary, His activity is always consistent with His nature. One of the most important statements about God in Scripture is that 'He cannot deny Himself'.[21] Does it come as a surprise that it is said God 'cannot' do something? Can He not do anything? Is He not omnipotent? Yes, He can do anything He pleases to do, anything which it is consistent with His nature to do. But His omnipotence does not mean that He can do absolutely anything whatsoever; for He limits it by His own self-consistency.

God's love and wrath, together with His works of salvation and of judgment, are sometimes set over against each other as supposedly incompatible. We have already mentioned how some people imagine the God of the Old Testament to be a God of anger and the God of the New Testament to be a God of mercy. But this is a false antithesis. The Old Testament also reveals Him as a God of mercy, while the New Testament also reveals Him as a God of judgment. Indeed the whole Bible, Old and New Testaments alike, presents Him as a God of love and wrath simultaneously. The Biblical authors are not embarrassed by this, as many moderns seem to be. Thus, the apostle John can tell his readers how 'God so loved the world that He gave His only Son' and at the end of the same chapter declare that on him who does not obey the Son 'the wrath of God rests'[22] Similarly, the apostle Paul can describe his readers as 'by nature the children of wrath, like the rest of mankind' and in the very next verse write that God is 'rich in mercy' and has loved us with a great love.[23]

The only explanation the Bible gives of the loving and wrathful activity of God, of His deeds of salvation and of judgment, is simply that He is like that. That is the kind of God He is, and this is why He acts that way. 'God is love', and therefore He loves the world and has given His Son for us.[24] But also 'our God is a consuming fire'.[25] His nature of perfect holiness can never compromise with evil but, as it were, 'devours' it. Always He sets Himself implacably against it.

One of the ways in which Scripture dares to express this truth of God's self-consistency is to say that He must and will 'satisfy Himself'.[26] That is to say, He is always perfectly Himself and acts in a way that is true to Himself. In every situation He expresses *Himself* as He is, in mercy and in judgment.

Having now drawn attention to the Biblical revelation of God as both living and sovereign on the one hand, and self-consistent on the other, there can be no doubt that the principal way in which the living God has expressed Himself is in 'grace'. No one can understand the message of Scripture, who does not know the meaning of grace. The God of the Bible is 'the God of all grace'.[27] Grace is love, but love of a special sort. It is love which stoops and sacrifices and serves, love which is kind to the unkind and generous to the ungrateful and undeserving. Grace is God's free and unmerited favour, loving the unlovable, seeking the fugitive, rescuing the hopeless,

166

and lifting the beggar from the dunghill to make him sit among princes.[28]

It is grace which led God to establish His covenant with a particular people. God's grace is covenant grace. True, it is also shown to everybody without distinction. This is called His 'common grace', by which He gives to all men indiscriminately such blessings as reason and conscience, love and beauty, life and food, marriage and children, work and leisure, ordered government and many other gifts besides. Yet God's entering into a special covenant with a special people may be described as His characteristic act of grace. For in it He took the initiative to choose out a people for Himself and to pledge Himself to be their God. He did not choose Israel because they were greater or better than other peoples. The reason for His choice lay in Him, not in them. As Moses explained it,

'The Lord has set His love upon you . . . because the Lord loves you'.[29]

'Covenant' is a legal term, and signifies any binding undertaking. When used in Scripture to describe what God has done, however, it is not to be thought of as an agreement between two equal parties, a kind of mutual contract. It is more like a 'testament' or will in which the testator has sole and entire discretion in the disposal of His own estate. Indeed, the English words 'covenant' and 'testament' can be used interchangeably, which is why the two halves of the Bible are known as the Old and New 'Testaments'. The Greek word *diathēkē* can mean either, and twice in the epistles there is a play on the two meanings of the word, in order to make it plain that God's covenant is like a 'last will and testament' in that He has freely made certain promises.[30] His covenant promises are not unconditional, since His people are

167

required to obey His commands and this is their part of the covenant, but God Himself lays down the commands as well as the promises. So even at Sinai God's covenant remains a covenant of grace.

It is important to grasp, then, that the covenant of God is the same throughout, from Abraham to Christ, so that those who are Christ's by faith are thereby Abraham's children and heirs of the promises God made him.[31] The law which was given at Sinai did not annul the covenant of grace. On the contrary, the covenant of grace was confirmed and renewed at Sinai. What the law did was to emphasize and expand the requirement of obedience. It is only when the law is considered in isolation from the covenant of grace that it is contrasted with the gospel. Then the law is seen to condemn the sinner for his disobedience, while the gospel offers him life by grace.

We are now in a position to think about what may be described as three stages in the outworking of God's covenant, expressed in the three words 'redemption', 'adoption' and 'glorification'.

Redemption

Redemption is originally not a theological but a commercial word. Often in the Old Testament (as today) we read about the redemption of land, which had been alienated from the owner's possession, or mortgaged. There were people also who needed to be redeemed, such as slaves and prisoners. In each case something or somebody was bought, in fact bought back from some state of alienation or bondage. To redeem was to purchase somebody's freedom, to recover by payment of a price something which had been lost.

This is the word which came to be applied to God's first act of grace towards His people. When they had somehow got lost, separated from Him and from their homeland in exile or captivity, He delivered them from their bondage and restored them to their land. This pattern repeated itself three times in Israel's history. First He called Abraham from Ur of the Chaldees (not, strictly speaking, a redemption because Abraham had not yet been in Canaan), then He delivered Israel from their Egyptian bondage and finally the exiles from their Babylonian captivity. In each He called, He acted, He delivered, and He brought them to the land of promise.

This is the Old Testament background to Jesus Christ's great work of redemption. Now man's alienation and bondage are spiritual. It is his sin—his rebellion against both his Creator's authority and his neighbour's welfare —which has enslaved him and separated him from God. And man in sin is man under judgment, deserving nothing for his revolt but death.

Into this situation of helplessness and despair came Jesus Christ. He took upon Him man's nature when He was born and man's guilt when He died. In the stark, unvarnished language of the New Testament He was first 'made flesh', and then 'made sin', even 'made a curse' for us.[32] For the simple truth is that He took our place. He identified Himself so completely with us in our predicament that He bore our sin and died our death. Our life was forfeit because of sin. He died instead of us, experiencing in our place the desolation of God-forsaken darkness.

The New Testament authors several times draw an analogy between the Passover, which initiated Israel's redemption from Egypt, and the death of Christ which has secured our redemption from sin. The life of every firstborn in Egypt was forfeit, but God made provision for the life of a lamb to be acceptable instead, if its blood was first shed and then sprinked on the lintel and sideposts of the front door. When God saw the blood, He passed over the house to protect it from His own judgment.

The New Testament fulfilment is dramatic. John showed in his Gospel that by one reckoning Jesus was shedding His blood on the cross at the precise time when the Passover lambs were being killed.[33] Paul wrote that 'Christ, our paschal (i.e. Passover) lamb, has been sacrificed',[34] while Peter referred to 'the precious blood of Christ, like that of a lamb without blemish or spot', which was shed to redeem us and must (symbolically, of course) be 'sprinkled' upon us.[35]

When Christ the Lamb of God had offered Himself as our Passover sacrifice, had shed his blood and died, God raised Him from the dead to vindicate Him, and to demonstrate that His sacrifice for sin had not been offered in vain. Now He is described as 'seated at God's right hand', resting from His finished work of redemption and crowned with glory and honour. He has won an 'eternal redemption'[36] for us. And throughout eternity the multitudes of heaven will sing 'Worthy is the Lamb who was slain . . .'[37]

Adoption

Redemption is a largely negative concept. It concentrates on the plight from which we have been delivered and on the price which had to be paid. True, to be redeemed from sin by Christ's blood is to be redeemed 'for God'.[38] But this positive aspect of our salvation is emphasized rather in the notion of our adoption to be His children. Paul brings the two together as virtually inseparable when he writes:

'When the time had fully come, God sent forth His Son, born of woman, born under the law, to redeem those who were under the law, so that we might receive adoption as sons. . . . So through God you are

170

no longer a slave but a son, and if a son then an heir.'[39]

Redeemed from slavery and adopted into sonship—
that is the glorious double privilege of those who put
their trust in Christ. Our relationship to God as His
children is an essential part of His covenant promise.

Already this fact of 'belonging to God' was plain in
Old Testament days. The covenant formula, used each
time the covenant was renewed, was 'I will be your God,
and you shall be My people'. Moreover, this adoption of
Israel to be the people of God immediately followed
their redemption. Again and again God had to remind
them of this, saying 'I am the Lord your God, who
brought you out of the land of Egypt, out of the house of
bondage'.[40] He had redeemed them. They were His. He
spelled it out very clearly to them during the period between their redemption from Egypt and the renewal of
the covenant at Sinai:

'You have seen what I did to the Egyptians, and how
I bore you on eagles' wings and brought you to Myself.
Now therefore, if you will obey My voice and keep
My covenant, you shall be My own possession among
all peoples; for all the earth is Mine, and you shall be
to Me a kingdom of priests and a holy nation . . .'[41]

Often this covenant, by which God's redeemed people
became His own possession, His special treasure, was
likened to a marriage covenant. Yahweh was the husband
of His people. He had delighted in His bride's early love
and devotion in the wilderness.[42] But in Canaan she went
after her 'lovers', the baals of the local shrines. She became
an adulteress, even a harlot. She broke the covenant.

The marriage metaphor is continued and expanded in
the New Testament. The apostle Paul described how
'Christ loved the church and gave Himself up for her',
but added how anxious He was—imbued even with

divine jealousy—lest this bride should be 'led astray from a sincere and pure devotion to Christ'.[43]

The relation between God and His people in New Testament days is expressed more often in terms of the Father and his family, however, than of the husband and his wife. It is a development of the Old Testament conviction that Israel was God's 'firstborn son'.[44] Jesus regularly taught His disciples to regard God as their heavenly Father and themselves as His beloved children, to pray to Him as their Father, to trust His fatherly care to supply their material needs, and to become concerned for their Father's name, kingdom and will.

One of the greatest privileges of being God's children is to have the Holy Spirit dwelling within us. The personal and abiding presence of the Holy Spirit in our hearts is a distinctive blessing, distinctive both of the Christian era itself,[45] and of the individual Christian. It is 'because we are sons' that 'God has sent the Spirit of His Son into our hearts'.[46] Paul enlarges on this:

'For all who are led by the Spirit of God are sons of God. For you did not receive the spirit of slavery to fall back into fear, but you have received the spirit of sonship. When we cry, "Abba! Father!" it is the Spirit Himself bearing witness with our spirit that we are children of God . . .'[47]

So the life of God's children may be described as 'life in the Spirit'. It is a life lived under the direction and by the power of the Holy Spirit. He bears witness with our spirit that we are indeed God's children. As the 'Spirit of wisdom and of revelation' in our knowledge of Christ,[48] He also opens the eyes of our heart to know Him better. And He is the *Holy* Spirit, seeking to lead us into *holiness*, to make us like Christ.[49] He subdues the power of our flesh (or fallen nature) and causes to ripen in our

172

character His fruit of 'love, joy, peace, patience, kindness, goodness, faithfulness, meekness and self-control'.[50]

The children of God together form His family, the church, enjoying a direct continuity with God's people in Old Testament days. This Christian brotherhood transcends all racial and social barriers. It is hard for us to imagine how great was 'the dividing wall of hostility' between Jew and Gentile. But Christ broke it down, and Paul devoted much of his Ephesian letter to the theme that Jews and Gentiles share in Christ on equal terms, being fellow-citizens of God's kingdom and fellow-members of God's family.[51]

Another great contemporary rift in society existed between those who were slaves and those who were free. In the Roman empire slaves had no rights before the law; all the privileges belonged to the free. But when Paul led to Christ a runaway slave called Onesimus, he sent him back to his master Philemon, begging him to welcome him 'no longer as a slave but more than a slave, as a beloved brother'.[52] The social effects of the gospel were explosive.

To sum up this unity, this equality, of all the members of God's family, Paul wrote:

'There is neither Jew nor Greek, there is neither slave nor free, there is neither male nor female; for you are all one in Christ Jesus.'[53]

This people of God is a 'holy' people, that is, a distinct or separate people, set apart from the rest of mankind to belong to God. Therefore they are called to be what they are, to manifest in their character and conduct the holiness of their status or position. They are 'called to be holy', that is, called to be different from the secular world, and not to be conformed to its outlook or standards. 'You shall not do as they do', God had said to Israel in the wilderness, referring both to the Egyptians and to the

173

Canaanites.[54] Similarly, 'do not be like them', Jesus said during the Sermon on the Mount, referring both to the Gentiles and to the Pharisees.

Instead, the Christian is to follow Christ. And His absolute ethical standards are set forth without compromise in both the Gospels and the Epistles, just as God's standards were set before Israel in the law and the prophets.

It must not be thought, however, that Christ's call to His people to be 'holy' or 'different' provides any excuse for withdrawal from the world into a pietistic isolation. On the contrary, the very same people whom Christ has 'chosen out of the world' He sends back 'into the world' as His representatives, to give themselves to other people in humble service and witness.[55]

Further, as they remain in the world for Christ, seeking to serve the world's needs but refusing to become assimilated to the world's standards, they will experience the world's opposition. The world will hate them for their very difference, Christ warned, and persecute them too.[56] So they will suffer. Indeed, to suffer unjustly and to forbear revenge is another part of the calling of Christians. For Christ left us an example of this, that we should follow in His footsteps.[57]

But suffering leads to glory. It was so for Christ. It is so for the followers of Christ. Peter commands us to rejoice both in our share of Christ's sufferings and in our anticipated share in the glory which is to be revealed.[58] The apostle Paul said the same thing:

'If children, then heirs, heirs of God and fellow-heirs with Christ, provided we suffer with Him in order that we may also be glorified with Him.'[59]

These are some of the implications of our 'adoption' into God's family. As children of our Father God, we are the dwelling place of His Spirit, united in brotherhood to all other Christian people, the ambassadors of Christ in the world, serving and suffering for His cause, and Christ's fellow-heirs as well.

For to be a son is to be an heir. Suffering is the pledge of glory. This leads us straight to the third stage in God's unfolding plan of salvation, 'glorification'.

Glorification

The New Testament is full of the Christian hope. It reminds us that, although in the past we have been redeemed from sin by Christ and are now enjoying the privileges of sonship which adoption into God's family has brought us, there is still far more to come. To this consummation we are eagerly looking forward. For our Christian 'hope' has no uncertainty about it. It is a joyful and confident expectation, based upon the promises of God. And it sustains us as we travel like pilgrims to our eternal home.

What is the object of our hope? To what are we looking forward? Paul called it 'the hope of glory'.[60] But what does this mean?

First, the return of Christ. It is not fashionable to believe in this today, or not in any literal sense. But Jesus clearly and repeatedly said He was going to come back, and that His return would be 'in power and great glory'. The apostles enlarged on this assurance. His coming will be personal and visible, although it will also have a transcendent quality which puts it beyond our present understanding:

'For as the lightning comes from the east and shines as far as the west, so will be the coming of the Son of man.'[61]

Secondly, the resurrection. Resurrection is not the same as resuscitation. Those whom Jesus raised from

175

death during His earthly ministry were resuscitated. They came back from death, resumed their former way of life, and then later died a second time. Resurrection, however, means the beginning of a new, a different, an immortal life. So our resurrected bodies, though retaining some kind of continuity with our present bodies, will also be changed. They will be as different, Paul says, as the plant is from the seed out of which it grows. They will be set free both from decay and from 'the flesh', the fallen nature which in some sense belongs to them. They will also have new powers. In fact our resurrection body will be a 'body of glory', like Christ's.[62]

Thirdly, the judgment. When Christ comes, both salvation and judgment will be brought to completion. For both are processes begun in this life, as Jesus made plain.[63] We shall be judged according to our works.[64] We cannot be justified (brought into acceptance with God) by our works; justification is only by God's grace through faith in Christ and His finished work. But we shall be judged by our works, because the judgment will be a public occasion, and our 'works'—what we have said and done—will be the only public evidence which can be adduced to prove the presence (or absence) of any saving faith. Those whose works reveal that they have disobeyed the gospel and rejected Christ will be lost. Whatever its precise nature may be, hell is a terrible reality. Christ called it 'outer darkness' and told us to fear God 'who can destroy both soul and body in hell'.[65]

Fourthly, the new universe. It is variously described. There will be 'a new heaven and a new earth',[66] for God will 'make all things new'.[67] Jesus called it 'the rebirth',[68] Paul the heading up or uniting of all things in Christ[69] and Peter the 'restoration of all things.'[70]

Popular Christian devotion has perhaps concentrated too much on the negative joys of heaven, that is, on the promises of the Revelation that there will be no more hunger or thirst, no more scorching heat or sunstroke, no more tears or pain, no more night, no more curse, no more death. Thank God for these absences. But thank God even more for their cause, namely the presence—the central, dominating presence—of the throne of God.

When John was granted his vision of heavenly reality, and was permitted to peer through 'an open door', the first thing on which his eye rested was 'a throne',[71] the symbol of God's sovereignty. Everything else in his vision was related to this throne. The Father sat on it, and the Lamb shared it, together with 'the seven spirits of God' representing the Holy Spirit. Round it in concentric circles were twenty-four elders symbolizing the church and four living creatures symbolizing the creation, and beyond them myriads of angels. Flashes of lightning and peals of thunder issued from the throne, and before the throne stood the great concourse of the redeemed, drawn from every nation and language, wearing white robes of righteousness, waving palm branches of victory, and ascribing their salvation to their God who sits on the throne and to the Lamb.[72]

The Bible begins with the creation of the universe and ends with the re-creation of the universe. It goes on at its beginning to describe the fall of man in a garden and paradise lost; it concludes in a garden, with paradise regained. Here are the tree of life for food and for healing, and the water of life for refreshment. And the river of the water of life is seen to be 'flowing from the throne of God and of the Lamb.'[73] For at last God's kingdom has been consummated. All creation is subject to Him. And the blessings of our final inheritance will be due to His perfect rule. So the great multitude sings:

'Hallelujah! For the Lord our God the Almighty reigns.'[74]

177

And somehow His redeemed, adopted, glorified people will share in His reign:

'They shall reign for ever and ever.'[75]

For Further Reading

The Message of the Old Testament by H. L. Ellison (Paternoster 1969, 94 pages). Described as 'a primer to the understanding of the Old Testament *as a whole*', this book is written in the conviction that the Old and the New Testament are each incomplete without the other. After an initial chapter on 'the Problem of the Old Testament' the author takes us chronologically through the Hebrew Bible, unfolding the message of the historical books, the law, the prophets, the psalter and the wisdom literature. Concise, but thorough.

Christian Beliefs (an introductory study guide) by I. Howard Marshall (IVP 2nd edition 1969, 94 pages). This pocketbook is intended 'for the newcomer to the study of Christian doctrine'. There are chapters on our knowledge of God, God and the universe, the person and work of Christ, the Christian life, the church and the last things. A very valuable summary. Each chapter ends with questions for discussion.

A Summary of Christian Doctrine by Louis Berkhof (1938, Banner of Truth edition 1960, 184 pages). Louis Berkhof, who died in 1957, came from a Dutch Reformed background and taught for many years at Calvin Theological Seminary, Grand Rapids, USA. His chapters on God, man, Christ, the application of redemption, the church and the last things are concise summaries of traditional reformed theology. Each chapter ends with questions both for review and for further study.

NOTES

1 Jn. 16.12–15
2 Is. 28.10
3 Heb. 1.1–2
4 James 1.17
5 Is. 46.3, 4
6 Ps. 115.4–7
7 Ps. 115.3
8 Ps. 95.5
9 Ps. 148.8
10 Ps. 29.10
11 Ps. 104.17, 18
12 Ps. 104.27, 28
13 Mt. 5.45; 6.26–30
14 Dan. 4.32
15 Ps. 99.1
16 Ps. 2.4
17 Acts 4.18, 23–28
18 Is. 10.5, 6
19 Jer. 25.9; 27.6
20 Is. 45.1–4 cf. 44.28
21 2 Tim. 2.13
22 Jn. 3.16, 36
23 Eph. 2.3, 4
24 1 Jn. 4.8, 9
25 Heb. 12.19 quoting Dt. 4.24
26 For verses in which God says He will 'spend', 'satisfy' or 'give full vent to' His anger and thus judge His people for their inveterate rebellion, see e.g. Ezck. 5.13 ff; 6.12; 7.8; 16.42, 43; 24.13, 14 and Lam. 4.11. In Psalm 89.33 ff, however, it is His steadfast love according to His covenant promise and oath which directs Him. 'I will not . . . be false to My faithfulness,' He says (v. 33). Cf. the declaration in Is. 53.11 that the Lord's suffering servant, seeing the fruit of His soul's travail, will 'be satisfied'.

27 1 Pet. 5.10
28 Ps. 113.7, 8
29 Dt. 7.7, 8
30 Gal. 3.15–18; Heb. 9.15–18
31 Gal. 3.29
32 Jn. 1.14; 2 Cor. 5.21; Gal. 3.13
33 Jn. 13.1; 18.28
34 1 Cor. 5.7
35 1 Pet. 1.2, 18, 19
36 Heb. 9.12
37 Rev. 5.12
38 Rev. 5.9
39 Gal. 4.4–7
40 Ex. 20.2
41 Ex. 19.4–6
42 Jer. 2.2; 31.32
43 Eph. 5.25; 2 Cor. 11.2, 3
44 e.g. Ex. 4.22
45 Jer. 31.33
46 Gal. 4.6
47 Rom. 8.14–16
48 Eph. 1.17
49 2 Cor. 3.18
50 Gal. 5.16–23
51 Eph. 2.19

52 Philem. 16
53 Gal. 3.28
54 Lev. 18.1–5
55 Jn. 15.19; 17.15–19
56 Jn. 15.18–25; 17.14
57 1 Pet. 2.18–23
58 1 Pet. 4.13; 5.1, 10
59 Rom. 8.17
60 Rom. 5.2
61 Mt. 24.27
62 see Phil. 3.21 and 1 Cor. 15.35–57
63 Jn. 5.19–29
64 Mt. 16.27; Jn. 5.28,29; Rom. 2.6; Rev. 20.11–15
65 Mt. 10.28
66 2 Pet. 3.13; Rev. 21.1
67 Rev. 21.5
68 Mt. 19.28, literally
69 Eph. 1.10
70 Acts 3.21, literally
71 Rev. 4.1, 2
72 Rev. 4–7
73 Rev. 22.1
74 Rev. 19.6
75 Rev. 22.5

6. THE AUTHORITY OF THE BIBLE

I tried in the previous chapter to summarize the message of the Bible, and in the previous chapters to outline both the geographical and the historical setting within which this message was received and recorded. But is the Biblical message what it purports to be, a revelation from God? Can we trust the Bible?

This question is crucial and cannot be dodged. Vital issues are at stake. For one thing, the Bible claims (as we have seen) to be a book of salvation, to 'instruct us for salvation'. Therefore we must know whether the way of salvation it unfolds is true or false. The eternal destiny of men depends upon it.

For another thing, the church of today is confused. The non-Christian world is constantly being treated to the unedifying spectacle of Christians in discord and disagreement. Why is this? The primary cause of confusion in the church is the lack of an agreed authority. Ultimately, of course, the church should submit to the authority of Christ, its Lord. But is it possible that Christ intends to rule and reform His church by His word? May it be that His exhortation 'He who has an ear, let him hear what the Spirit says to the churches'[1] is an invitation to listen to *Scripture* through which the Spirit still speaks to the church?

For these two reasons at least our enquiry as to whether and why the Bible has authority is of great practical importance.

Yet it is also at variance with the contemporary mood. Strong anti-authoritarian tides are running. There is a prevalent revolt against all established authority, of both institutions and traditions. If we could demonstrate that the Bible has authority, many people would on that account be more ready to reject than to accept it. In addition, it is fashionable nowadays to indulge in a little religious syncretism, that is, to deny to every religion whatever exclusive elements it may claim, to assert that all religions are relatively true and so to try to combine them. Other religions also have their holy books; what is so special about the Christian Scriptures, the Bible?

Three Definitions

Aware, then, of the importance of our subject and of the disfavour with which many will regard our attempt to defend the uniqueness of the Bible, we shall begin with some definitions. The three great words commonly used by Christians in this connection are 'revelation', 'inspiration' and 'authority'. They are related but distinct.

The fundamental word is 'revelation'. Derived from a Latin noun meaning 'unveiling', it indicates that God has taken the initiative to make Himself known. The reasonableness of this concept should be plain. For whoever or whatever God may be, He is altogether beyond our ken. 'Can you find out the deep things of God? Can you find out the limit of the Almighty?'.[2] Indeed, not. His infinite greatness is veiled from our eyes. We cannot discover Him by ourselves. If we are ever to know Him, He must make Himself known.

The second word 'inspiration' indicates the chief mode God has chosen by which to reveal Himself. He has revealed Himself partly in nature and supremely in Christ, but also by 'speaking' to particular people. And it is this process of verbal communication which is called 'inspiration'. We do not use it in the general sense that we may say a poet or musician is 'inspired'. On the contrary, it has a special and precise connotation. For when Paul writes that 'all Scripture is inspired by God',[3] the last three words represent a single Greek expression which would be literally translated 'God-breathed'. The meaning, then, is not that God breathed into the writers, nor that He somehow breathed into the writings to give them their special character, but that what was written by men was breathed out by God. He spoke through them. They were His spokesmen.

Further, we do not hesitate to say that this inspiration was 'verbal inspiration', in that it extended to the very words used by the human authors. This is what they claimed. The apostle Paul, for example, could declare that in communicating to others what God had revealed to him, he used 'words not taught by human wisdom but taught by the Spirit'.[4] Nor is this in the least surprising, for it is not possible to convey a precise message in any other way than in precise words.

'Authority', the third word, is the power or weight which inheres in Scripture because of what it is, namely a divine revelation given by divine inspiration. If it is a word from God, it has authority over men. For behind every word that anybody utters stands the person who speaks it. It is the speaker himself (his character, knowledge and position) who determines how people regard his words. So God's word carries God's authority. It is because of who He is that we believe what He has said.

This is the lesson Simon Peter learned when Jesus told him on the lake of Galilee to put out into the deep and let down his nets for a catch. All his fisherman's expertise, gathered from years of experience, rebelled against the suggestion. He even protested, 'Master, we toiled all night and took nothing!'. Yet wisely he added 'But at Your word I will let down the nets.'[5]

Our claim, then, is that God has revealed Himself by speaking; that this divine (or God-breathed) speech has been written down and preserved in Scripture; and that Scripture is, in fact, God's word written, which therefore is true and reliable and has divine authority over men.

Three Disclaimers

It seems necessary now to add to these definitions certain disclaimers which may anticipate objections and disarm possible criticism.

First, the process of inspiration was not a mechanical one. God did not treat the human authors of Scripture as dictating machines or tape recorders, but as living and responsible persons. Sometimes He spoke to them in dreams and visions, sometimes by an audible voice, sometimes by angels. At other times we are not told how the word of God came to them. They may well not have been conscious of it at all. Thus in the case of Luke the evangelist divine inspiration was certainly not incompatible with human research, for he tells us in the preface to his Gospel about the painstaking enquiries he had pursued. Whatever means of communication God employed in speaking to men, it never obliterated their own personality. On the contrary, as they wrote, their literary style and vocabulary were their own. So too— more important still—was their theme. It is not an accident that Amos was the prophet of God's justice, Hosea of His love and Isaiah of His kingly sovereignty, nor that Paul was the apostle of grace and faith, James of works, John of love, and Peter of hope. The internal evidence, culled from reading the Biblical text, is that God made full use of the personality, temperament, background and experience of the Biblical authors, in order to convey through each an appropriate and distinctive message.

So then Scripture is equally the word of God and the word of men. This is, indeed, how it describes itself. If it is true that 'the mouth of the Lord has spoken,'[6] it is also true that 'God spoke by the mouth of his holy prophets.'[7] Similarly, 'God spoke . . . through the prophets,[8] and 'men . . . spoke from God'.[9] Again, the law could be described by the same author in the same passage as both 'the law of Moses' and 'the law of the Lord'.[10]

The dual authorship of Scripture is an important truth to be carefully guarded. On the one hand, *God* spoke, revealing the truth and preserving the human authors from error, yet without violating their personality. On the other hand, *men* spoke, using their own faculties freely, yet without distorting the divine message. Their words were truly their own words. But they were (and still are) also God's words, so that what Scripture says, God says.

My second disclaimer is that, although Scripture as God's word is true, this does not mean—to quote a common claim—that 'every word of the Bible is literally true.' Such a statement would need to be qualified in several ways. Although I am here trespassing slightly upon what I shall write in the next chapter about Biblical interpretation, I think I need to say something about it here.

To begin with, every word of the Bible is true only in its context. Isolated from its context, it may be quite untrue. The best example of what I mean is the Book of

Job, the bulk of which consists of a dialogue between the grief-stricken Job and his three 'comforters', together with a fourth who appears later. This occupies chapters 1 to 37. Then God reveals Himself to Job in chapters 38 to 42. Some of what Job and his comforters say about suffering in the first 37 chapters is mistaken. It is recorded in order to be contradicted, not in order to be believed. We are told so at the end of the book when Job says to God 'I have uttered what I did not understand' and God says to his comforters 'you have not spoken of Me what is right.'[11] It would be quite impossible, therefore, to take any verse from the Book of Job and say 'this is the word of God', for it may not be. The book as a whole is God's word, but the first 37 chapters can be understood only in the light of the last 5.

Then again much of Scripture is deliberately presented in a highly figurative manner. Thus, there are many 'anthropomorphic' descriptions of God, representing Him in human form, and referring to His eyes and ears, His 'outstretched arm', 'mighty hand' and fingers, His mouth, His breath and His nostrils. We do not interpret these *literally*, for the simple reason that 'God is spirit'[12] and therefore has no body. So when we read that 'the eyes of the Lord run to and fro throughout the whole earth, to show His might in behalf of those whose heart is blameless toward Him,'[13] we do not try to visualize a pair of divine eyes running about over the earth's surface, but understand rather that God sees everyone everywhere and is always ready to save those who trust in Him. In the same way, when we read of people hiding under His 'wings', we do not picture Him as a bird with feathers, but learn that He protects those who take refuge in Him.

Similarly, when the Psalmist writes that the sun 'comes forth like a bridegroom leaving his chamber, and like a strong man runs its course with joy', and when he goes on to refer to the sun's 'rising' and 'circuit' from one end of the heavens to the other,[14] he does not commit us to a pre-Copernican view of the solar system. For he is evidently describing the sun's resplendent magnificence both in poetic imagery and from the point of view of an earth-bound observer. Even sophisticated technocrats of the 1970s can wax eloquent about the sun, and can talk of its 'rising' and 'setting'. They do not need to apologize for doing so. Men recognize that they are using the language of poetry, and of ordinary observation, not of science.

The third disclaimer I would make concerns what the inspired text of Scripture is, which alone can be regarded as God's word written. This is the original Hebrew or Greek text as it came from the authors' hands. We claim no special inspiration or authority for any particular translation—whether ancient Latin or modern English, nor indeed for any particular interpretation.

It is true that no actual autograph has survived. Their loss is presumably due to a deliberate providence of God, which may have been to prevent men giving superstitious reverence to pieces of paper. Nevertheless, we know something of the scrupulous care with which scribes copied the sacred Hebrew text, and the same will have been true of the New Testament documents. Further, we possess far more early copies of the original text than of any other ancient literature. By comparing these with each other, with the early 'versions' (i.e. translations) and with Biblical quotations in the writings of the church fathers, scholars (so called 'textual critics') have been able to establish the authentic text (especially of the New Testament) beyond any reasonable doubt. The uncertainties which remain are almost entirely trivial; no doctrine of any importance hangs upon them.

So far I have tried to clear the ground by indicating both what we do and what we do not claim for the Bible. It is now time to ask on what grounds we base our assurance that it is God's word written, originating with God and authoritative for men. Many different answers have been given. I will touch on the first three briefly and concentrate on the fourth and decisive argument.

Arguments for the Authority of Scripture

The first point to make is that the historic Christian churches have consistently maintained and defended the divine origin of Scripture. Only in comparatively recent times have some churches changed their official doctrine on this matter. Whether we consult the formularies of Roman, Anglican, Presbyterian, Lutheran or other churches, the witness is virtually unanimous. Now this is not a conclusive argument and may not appeal at all to some. Nevertheless, the tradition of the centuries is not to be lightly set aside or despised, and the consensus on this matter is very impressive.

Secondly, we turn from what the historic churches have consistently taught to what the Biblical writers themselves claimed. This is even more impressive. For example, Moses said he received the law from God. The prophets introduced their oracles with formulae like 'Thus says the Lord' or 'The word of the Lord came to me, saying'. And the apostles could write such statements as this one from Paul:

'When you received the word of God which you heard from us, you accepted it not as the word of men but as what it really is, the word of God, which is at work in you believers.'[15]

The Biblical authors also made similar claims for each other. We find in Scripture an elaborate pattern of cross-authorization. For example, the prophets endorsed the law, and the psalmists extolled its truth, beauty and sweetness.[16] Above all, the New Testament confirms the

Old, the apostolic authors drawing from it a rich variety of quotations as divine warrant for what they were writing. There is even the famous passage in which the apostle Peter refers to the letters of 'our beloved brother Paul,' comments on the 'wisdom' given to him and equates his epistles with Scripture.[17]

The third line of evidence for the inspiration and authority of Scripture is supplied not by the writers but by the readers of Scripture. For there are certain characteristics of the Bible which cannot fail to strike the observant reader. There is, for instance, the book's remarkable unity and coherence, on which I have tried to enlarge in earlier chapters. In view of the diversity of human authorship, the best explanation of this unity seems to be the overshadowing activity of a single divine author behind the human authors. There is also, as one aspect of this overall unity, the striking phenomenon of fulfilled prophecy. Then there are the nobility and dignity of the great themes of Scripture and the extraordinary relevance of its message thousands of years later, to which its continuing popularity bears witness.

Further, there is the power which the Bible has had (God's power through it, we believe) in human lives, disturbing the complacent and comforting the sorrowful, abasing the proud, reforming the sinful, encouraging the faint-hearted, bringing hope to the bereaved and giving direction to those who have lost their way. Added to all this is what the Reformers called 'the inward witness of the Holy Spirit'. It is the deep assurance that Scripture is truth from God, an assurance arising not from external confirmation such as archaeological discoveries (helpful as these are), but internally from the Holy Spirit Himself. It is the experience of the 'burning heart', given first to the disciples on the Emmaus Road, but still granted to Christian disciples of the modern world:

'Did not our hearts burn within us while He talked to us on the road, while He opened to us the Scriptures.'[18]

However, the first and foremost reason why Christians believe in the divine inspiration and authority of Scripture is not because of what the churches teach, the writers claimed or the readers sense, but because of what Jesus Christ Himself said. Since He endorsed the authority of Scripture, we are bound to conclude that His authority and Scripture's authority either stand or fall together.[19]

Some may at once retort that to rely on Christ's witness to Scripture is to employ a circular argument, which might be expressed like this: 'How do I know that Scripture is inspired? Because of Christ, who says so. How do I know that Christ says so? Because of Scripture, which is inspired.' This, our critics point out, is to beg the question. For it is to assume the very truth we are wanting to prove. But they have misstated our argument. When we make our first approach to the Bible, we bring with us no assumptions about its divine inspiration. We accept it merely as a collection of historical documents, containing in particular the witness of first century Christians to Christ. As we read their testimony, we come to believe in Christ, still without formulating any particular doctrine of Scripture. But then the Christ we have come to believe in sends us back to Scripture. He gives us a new understanding of it because He endorses its authority for us.

But how did Christ endorse Scripture? Scripture consists, of course, of two separate halves, the Old and the New Testaments. And the way in which Jesus Christ set His seal on each is different.

Christ's view of the Old Testament

Take the Old Testament first. There can be no doubt, as any careful readers of the Gospels will agree, that Jesus gave His reverent assent to the authority of Old Testament Scripture, for He submitted to its authority Himself. I will give three examples to demonstrate this.

First, Jesus submitted to the Old Testament in His personal conduct. Thus, He countered each of the temptations of the devil by an apt Biblical quotation. It is sometimes said that He quoted Scripture 'at the devil'. This is not so. It would be more accurate to say that He quoted Scripture at Himself in the presence of the devil. For when the devil offered Him the kingdoms of the world if He would fall down and worship him, Jesus replied:

'Begone, Satan! For it is written, "You shall worship the Lord your God and Him only shall you serve" '.[20]

Jesus was not applying this text to Satan, but to Himself. He knew from Scripture that worship was due to God alone. Therefore He would obey. As man He would worship God, not Satan. The simple word *gegraptai* ('it stands written') was enough for Him. There was no need to question, discuss, argue or negotiate. The matter had already been settled by Scripture. This voluntary, personal submission of God's Son to the authority of God's word is extremely significant.

Secondly, Jesus submitted to the Old Testament in the fulfilment of His mission. He seems to have come to an understanding of His Messianic role from a study of Old Testament Scripture. He knew Himself to be both Isaiah's suffering servant and Daniel's son of man. So He accepted that He could enter into His glory only by the road of suffering and death. This explains the sense of necessity, of compulsion which constrained Him:

'The son of man must suffer many things and be rejected . . . and be killed, and after three days rise again.'[21]

191

Why 'must'? Because the Scripture said so. Voluntarily and deliberately He put Himself under the authority of what stood written, and He determined to fulfil it, in His mission as in His conduct. So when Peter tried to avert His arrest in the Garden of Gethsemane, He told Peter to sheathe his sword. He had no need of human defence. Could He not appeal to His Father for legions of defending angels? Then why did He not do so? Here is the reason He gave:

> 'How then should the Scriptures be fulfilled, that it must be so?'[22]

He was of the same opinion after the resurrection, and confirmed it both to the two Emmaus disciples and to the wider group of His followers:

> 'Was it not necessary that the Christ should suffer these things and enter into His glory? These are My words which I spoke to you, while I was still with you, that everything written about Me in the law of Moses and the prophets and the psalms must be fulfilled.'[23]

Thirdly, Jesus submitted to the Old Testament in His controversies. He found Himself engaged in continuous debate with the religious leaders of His day, and whenever there was a difference of opinion between them, He regarded Scripture as the only court of appeal. 'What is written in the law?' He would ask. 'How do you read?'[24] Again, 'Have you not read this Scripture. . . . ?'[25] One of His chief criticisms of His contemporaries concerned their disrespect for Scripture. The Pharisees added to it and the Sadducees subtracted from it. So to the Pharisees He said:

> 'You have a fine way of rejecting the commandment of God, in order to keep your tradition! . . . making void the word of God through your tradition which you hand on.'[26]

And to the Sadducees:

'Is not this why you are wrong, that you know neither the Scriptures nor the power of God?'[27]

It is beyond question, then, that Jesus Christ was Himself personally submissive to Scripture. In His own ethical standards, in His understanding of His mission, and in debate with the Jewish leaders, what the Scripture said was decisive for Him. 'Scripture cannot be broken', He affirmed.[28] And again,

'Truly, I say to you, till heaven and earth pass away, not an iota, not a dot, will pass from the law until all is accomplished.'[29]

There is no example of Christ contradicting the divine origin of Old Testament Scripture. Some people have supposed that He did so in the six antitheses of the Sermon on the Mount, in which He said 'You have heard that it was said . . ., but I say to you . . .'. However, it is not Moses with whom He was at odds, but the scribal perversions of Moses; not Scripture (which is God's word), but tradition (which is man's). All the available evidence confirms that Jesus Christ assented in His mind and submitted in His life to the authority of Old Testament Scripture. Is it not inconceivable that His followers should have a lower view of it than He?

Christ's Provision for the New Testament

Christ's way of endorsing the New Testament was, of course, different from His way of endorsing the Old, for none of the books of the New Testament had yet been written. If then the writing of the New Testament belonged entirely to the future, how could He endorse it at all?

The answer to this question lies in His appointment of the apostles. Jesus seems to have foreseen the need for Scriptures of the New Testament corresponding to the Scriptures of the Old. In the Old Testament God was active in redeeming and judging Israel, and Himself raised up prophets to give a true record and interpretation of what He was doing. Now God was active, through Christ, in redeeming and judging the world. Was this supreme and final revelation of God in Christ to be lost to future generations? No, there must be authoritative scribes and interpreters for this revelation as well. So Jesus made provision for this very thing. He carefully (after a whole night of prayer) chose and appointed, and then went on to train and authorize, the twelve apostles to be His witnesses, as God had chosen the prophets in Old Testament days:

'In those days He went out into the hills to pray; and all night He continued in prayer to God. And when it was day, He called His disciples, and chose from them twelve, whom He named apostles.'[30]

All the followers of Jesus were 'disciples'; only the twelve were named 'apostles'. A study of the New Testament use of the title shows that, although there were 'apostles of the churches' roughly equivalent to modern missionaries,[31] 'the apostles of Christ' were a small and restricted circle consisting of the Twelve, Matthias (who replaced Judas), Paul, James the Lord's brother, and perhaps one or two others. Although the whole church is apostolic in the sense that Christ sends it into the world on His mission, and although every Christian should be involved in this mission, yet 'apostle' is not a general word for a Christian in the New Testament. Even Paul's loyal and trusted colleagues like Timothy were not apostles. He deliberately drew a distinction between himself and them. Thus, he began his

194

letter to the Colossians: 'Paul, an apostle of Christ Jesus by the will of God, and Timothy our brother'. Timothy was a brother. Indeed, all Christians are brothers. But he was not an apostle of Christ like Paul.

Modern research suggests that the Greek word *apostolos* is the equivalent of the Aramaic *shaliach*, and that the *shaliach* in Rabbinic Judaism was a person with a clearly defined role. He was an emissary of the Sanhedrin, sent out to the Jews of the dispersion to teach in the Council's name. It was said of him: 'the one sent by a person is as this person himself'. In other words, he was a plenipotentiary, speaking with the authority of the person or body that had commissioned him. Thus Saul of Tarsus went to the synagogues at Damascus, armed 'with the authority and commission of the chief priests'.[32]

It is against this background that Jesus chose twelve men and deliberately gave them this title. The apostles were to be His personal representatives, endowed with His authority to speak in His name. When He sent them out, He said to them, 'He who receives you receives Me.'[33]

The apostles of Jesus appear to have had a fourfold uniqueness.

First, they had a personal call and authorization by Christ. This was clear in the case of the Twelve, and Paul claimed something comparable. He vehemently asserted and defended his apostolic authority, insisting that he had received his commission to be an apostle 'not from men nor through man, but through Jesus Christ and God the Father'.[34] It is further significant that in one of the accounts of Paul's conversion which Luke gives in the Acts, we are told the very words which Jesus used to commission him, namely *ego apostello se*, 'I send you' or 'I make you an apostle.'[35]

Secondly, they had an eye-witness experience of Christ. The twelve were appointed, Mark says, 'to be with Him, and to be sent out to preach'.[36] The verb 'sent out' is again *apostellein*, and their essential qualification for the work of apostleship was to be 'with Him'. Similarly, shortly before He died, Jesus said to them:

'You also are witnesses, because you have been with Me from the beginning.'[37]

So He gave them unrivalled opportunities to hear His words and see His works, so that they might later bear witness to what they had seen and heard.[38] Especially was it important for them to be witnesses of His resurrection. It was for this that Matthias was chosen, 'to take the place in this ministry and apostleship from which Judas turned aside'.[39]

It is true, of course, that Paul was not one of the original twelve, that he did not have the eye-witness experience of Christ which they had, and that probably he never even saw Christ in the flesh. Some have conjectured that the three years he spent in Arabia, during which he says he received his gospel 'through a revelation of Jesus Christ',[40] were deliberately intended to compensate him for the three years of Christ's public ministry which he had missed. Be that as it may, he fulfilled this second apostolic qualification by being a witness of the resurrection. 'Am I not an apostle?' he cried; 'have I not seen Jesus our Lord?'[41] His reference is of course to his encounter with Christ on the Damascus Road. Although it took place after the Ascension, nevertheless he claims that it was an actual, objective resurrection appearance, and he adds that it was the last. At the end of his catalogue of the resurrection appearances he writes:

'Last of all, as to one untimely born, He appeared also to me. For I am the least of the apostles . . .'[42]

Thirdly, they had an extraordinary inspiration of the Holy Spirit. We saw in the previous chapter that the in-

196

dwelling and illumination of the Holy Spirit is the privilege of all God's children. This privilege was not restricted to the apostles. Nevertheless, the ministry of the Spirit which Christ promised the apostles was something quite unique, as should be clear from these words:

> 'These things I have spoken to you, while I am still with you. But the Counsellor, the Holy Spirit, whom the Father will send in My name, He will teach you all things, and bring to your remembrance all that I have said to you. . . .
>
> 'I have yet many things to say to you, but you cannot bear them now. When the Spirit of truth comes, He will guide you into all the truth . . .'[43]

These wonderful promises have sometimes been applied to all Christian people. Doubtless they do have a secondary reference to us all. But their primary reference is evidently to the apostles who were gathered round Christ in the Upper Room, of whom He could say 'These things I have spoken to you while I am still with you' and 'I have yet many things to say to you, but you cannot bear them now.'

What He promised them was twofold. First, that the Holy Spirit would remind them of the teaching He had given them, and secondly that He would supplement it, leading them into all the truth which they could not at the moment bear. The major fulfilment of these promises was in the writing of the gospels and the epistles of the New Testament.

Fourthly, they had the power to work miracles. The Book of Acts is rightly called 'The Acts of the Apostles',[44] and Paul designates the 'signs and wonders and mighty works' which he had performed 'the signs of a true apostle'.[45] Further, the purpose of the miraculous power given to the apostles was to authenticate their apostolic commission and message:

197

'How shall we escape if we neglect such a great salvation? It was declared at first by the Lord (i.e. the Lord Jesus), and it was attested to us by those who heard Him (i.e. the apostolic eye-witnesses), while God also bore witness by signs and wonders and various miracles and by gifts of the Holy Spirit distributed according to His own will.'[46]

In these four ways the apostles seem to have been unique.

The Apostles' Authority Confirmed

Our impression of the uniqueness of the apostles is confirmed in two ways. First, they themselves knew it, and so exhibit in the New Testament their self-conscious apostolic authority. This is certainly so of Paul and John. Paul not only defends his authority as an apostle (as we have seen); he asserts it. Listen to the dogmatic instructions he gave the Thessalonian Church:

'We have confidence in the Lord about you, that you are doing and will do the things which we command. . . . Now we command you, brethren, in the name of our Lord Jesus Christ . . . For even when we were with you, we gave you this command . . . Now such persons we command and exhort in the Lord Jesus Christ. . . . If anyone refuses to obey what we say in this letter . . .'[47]

Who is this 'we'? It is the plural of apostolic authority. And who is it who presumes to issue these authoritative commands and to demand obedience? Again, it is an apostle of Christ, who speaks in the name of Christ. He claims that Christ was speaking in and through him.[48] As a result, when he first visited Galatia, although he was disfigured by illness, the Galatians did not scorn or despise him, but actually received him 'as an angel of God, as Christ Jesus'.[49] Paul does not rebuke them for paying him an exaggerated deference. On the contrary, they were right to receive him thus, for he was an apostle, an ambassador, an authorized representative of Jesus Christ.

John also used the plural of apostolic authority[50] and constantly recalled his readers to the original teaching he had given them. In view of the prevalence of false teachers he dared even to write:

'We are of God. Whoever knows God listens to us, and he who is not of God does not listen to us. By this we know the spirit of truth and the spirit of error.'[51]

In other words, a safe test by which John's readers could discern between truth and error was whether it was in accord with his teaching. False teachers would show their falsity by not listening to John, while the true Christian would authenticate himself by his submission to the apostle's authority.

The second way in which the unique authority of the apostles is substantiated is that the early church recognized it. For example, in the post-apostolic period, round about 110 A.D., soon after John the last apostle had died, Bishop Ignatius of Antioch sent letters to several churches of Asia Minor and Europe. In his *Epistle to the Romans* (ch. 4), he wrote:

'I do not, as Peter and Paul, issue commandments unto you. They were apostles; I am but a condemned man.'

He was a bishop. But he recognized that even a bishop's authority was not comparable to an apostle's.

When in the fourth century the church came finally to settle which books should be included in the New Testament canon and which excluded, the test they applied was whether a book came from the apostles. That is, was it written by an apostle? If not, did it emanate from the circle of the apostles and carry the endorsement of their authority? It is important to add this, for not every New Testament book was written by an apostle. But it seems to have been recognized that if a non-apostolic document nevertheless carried a kind of apostolic imprimatur, it should be recognized as 'apostolic'. For example, Luke was known to have been a regular companion and colleague of Paul, and Mark was described by the early church fathers Papias and Irenaeus as 'the interpreter of Peter' who faithfully recorded Peter's memories of Christ and the substance of his preaching.[52] Thus, the church was in no sense conferring authority on the canonical books; it was simply recognizing the authority they already possessed.

It is time now to summarize the argument which has been developed. Christ endorsed the authority of the Old Testament. He also made provision for the New Testament by authorising His apostles to teach in His name. Therefore if we would bow to Christ's authority, we must bow to Scripture's. It is because of Jesus Christ that Christians submit to both Old and New Testaments.

What are the alternatives to this conclusion? There are only two.

The first is to say that Christ was mistaken in His view of Scripture. In this case the argument would run somewhat as follows: 'The incarnation imprisoned Jesus in the limited mentality of a first-century Jew. Of course He accepted the authority of Scripture, for this is what the Jews of His day believed. But that is no reason why we should. Their view and His are outmoded'. This is the so-called theory of 'kenosis', from the Greek word which declares that He 'emptied Himself'[53] when He became man. He certainly emptied Himself of His glory when He took the form of a servant. But He did not empty

Himself of His deity in becoming man. And although as man He seems to have been ignorant of certain matters (He said He did not know the day of His return[54]), the remarkable fact is that He was not ignorant of His ignorance. He knew the limits of His knowledge. Consequently in His instruction He never strayed beyond these limits. On the contrary, He insisted that He taught only what the Father gave Him to teach.[55] Therefore we claim that He was inerrant, that all His teaching was true, including His endorsement of the authority of Scripture.

The second alternative which has been proposed may be expressed like this: 'Jesus knew perfectly well that Scripture was not entirely the word of God and reliable. Yet because His contemporaries all believed that it was, He accommodated Himself to their position. There is no need for us to do so.' But this suggestion is quite intolerable. It is derogatory to Christ, and incompatible with His claim to be the truth, and teach the truth. Besides, He never hesitated to disagree with His contemporaries on other matters, so why should He have done so on this? Further, this reconstruction would attribute to Jesus the very thing He detested most—religious pretense, or hypocrisy.

So we reject both the 'kenosis' and the 'accommodation' theories. Over against them we must insist that Jesus knew what He was talking about, and that He meant it. He taught knowledgeably, deliberately and with entire sincerity. He declared the divine origin of all Scripture for the straightforward reason that He believed it. And what He believed and taught is true.

Some Conclusions

In conclusion, let me emphasize both the rightness and the reasonableness of submitting to the authority of Scripture.

First, to accept the authority of the Bible is a Christian thing to do. It is neither a religious eccentricity, nor a case of discreditable obscurantism, but the good sense of Christian faith and humility. It is essentially 'Christian' because it is what Christ Himself requires of us. The traditional view of Scripture (that it is God's word written) is the Christian view of Scripture precisely because it is Christ's view of Scripture.

Secondly, what shall we do with the problems? To accept the divine origin of the Bible is not to pretend that there are no problems. To be candid, there are many problems—literary, historical, theological and moral. So what shall we do with them? Is it compatible with intellectual integrity to accept the unique authority of Scripture when so many residual problems surround it? Yes indeed it is.

We need to learn to do with the problems surrounding Scripture exactly what we do with the problems surrounding any other Christian doctrine. Every Christian doctrine has its problems. No doctrine is entirely free of them. Take as an example the doctrine of the love of God. Every Christian of every conceivable hue believes that God is love—Roman, Orthodox, Anglican, Reformed, Lutheran, Baptist, Brethren. It is a fundamental Christian doctrine. To disbelieve this is to disqualify oneself as a Christian. But the problems surrounding the doctrine are massive. What, then, do we do when someone brings us a problem touching God's love, a problem of evil or of undeserved suffering, for instance? In the first place, we shall wrestle with the problem and we may be granted some fresh light on it. But we are not likely to solve it altogether. So then what? Must we abandon our belief in the love of God until we have solved all the problems? No. We shall maintain our belief in the love of God, in spite of the problems, for one reason and for one reason only, namely that Jesus Christ taught it and

202

exhibited it. That is why we believe that God is love. And the problems do not overthrow our belief.

So with Scripture. Someone brings us a problem, maybe an apparent discrepancy or a question of literary criticism. What shall we do? To begin with, we shall wrestle with the problem, and perhaps find fresh light on it. But we may well not entirely solve it. So then what? Must we abandon our belief in the Word of God until we have solved all the problems? No. We shall maintain our belief in God's Word, just as we maintain our belief in God's love, in spite of the problems, ultimately for one reason and for one reason only, namely that Jesus Christ taught it and exhibited it. It is no more obscurantist to cling to the one belief than the other. Indeed, it is not obscurantist at all. To follow Christ is always sober, humble, Christian realism.

Thirdly, the ultimate issue in the question of authority concerns the lordship of Christ. 'You call Me Teacher and Lord', He said, 'and you are right; for so I am'.[56] If Jesus Christ is truly our teacher and our lord, we are under both His instruction and His authority. We must therefore bring our mind into subjection to Him as our teacher and our will into subjection to Him as our lord. We have no liberty to disagree with Him or to disobey Him. So we bow to the authority of Scripture because we bow to the authority of Christ.

For Further Reading

God Has Spoken (Revelation and the Bible) by J. I. Packer (Hodder and Stoughton 1965, 96 pages). After an introductory chapter deploring the present disastrous 'famine' of hearing God's word, because of the wrong turning taken by Biblical criticism, Dr. Packer writes of 'God's Word spoken' (that His revelation was given in words, and is therefore 'propositional' as well as 'personal'), 'God's Word written' (the authority, interpretation and sufficiency of Scripture) and 'God's Word heard' (leading to a Christian life of faith and obedience). This little book belongs to an Anglican series called *Christian Foundations*, but is a stirring summons to all Christian people and contains a penetrating critique of modern liberal views.

Our Lord's View of the Old Testament by J. W. Wenham, (Tyndale 1953, 32 pages). A thorough and convincing study of the Gospels to show that Jesus accepted the historical truth, the authority and the inspiration of Old Testament Scripture.

Supreme Authority by Norval Geldenhuys (Marshall, Morgan & Scott 1953, 128 pages). The late Norval Geldenhuys, a minister of the Dutch Reformed Church in South Africa, presents his readers with a cogent statement of the authority (a) of the Lord Jesus Himself (b) of His apostles and, consequently, (c) of the New Testament. Although Hebrew and Greek words are not transliterated into English, the non-professional student should derive as much profit from this book as the theologian. The fundamental issue he develops is the lordship of Christ.

The New Testament Documents: Are They Reliable? by F. F. Bruce (IVF first published 1943, 122 pages). Professor Bruce is concerned in this paperback rather with the historical reliability of the New Testament, than with its theological truth. Alongside general chapters on dating, attestation, archaeology and external evidence, he has more specific chapters on the canon, the miracles, the Gospels and the writings of Paul and Luke. An invaluable summary.

NOTES

1 Rev. 2 and 3
2 Job 11.7
3 2 Tim. 3.16
4 1 Cor. 2.13
5 Lk. 5.4, 5
6 e.g. Is. 1.20
7 e.g. Acts 3.21
8 Heb. 1.1
9 2 Pet. 1.21
10 Lk. 2.22, 23
11 Job 42.3, 7
12 Jn. 4.24
13 2 Chron. 16.9
14 Ps. 19.1–6
15 1 Thess. 2.13
16 e.g. Ps. 19 and 119
17 2 Pet. 3. 15, 16
18 Lk. 24.32
19 For a fuller treatment
   of this theme see the
   author's chapter 2 in
   Guidelines (Falcon 1967),
   entitled 'Jesus Christ our
   Teacher and Lord—
   towards solving the
   problem of authority'
20 Mt. 4.10
21 Mk. 8.31
22 Mt. 26.54
23 Lk. 24.26, 44
24 Lk. 10.26
25 Mk. 12.10
26 Mk. 7.9, 13
27 Mk. 12.24
28 Jn. 10.35
29 Mt. 5.18
30 Lk. 6.12, 13
31 e.g. 2 Cor. 8.23; Acts
   13.1–3; 14.14; Phil. 2.25
32 Acts 26.12.cf. 9.1, 2 and
   22.5
33 Mt. 10.40; Jn. 13.20
34 Gal. 1.1
35 Acts 26.17 cf. 22.21
36 Mk. 3.14
37 Jn. 15.27
38 cf. 1 Jn. 1.1–3
39 Acts. 1.21–26
40 Gal. 1.11, 12, 17, 18
41 1 Cor. 9.1
42 1 Cor. 15.8, 9
43 Jn. 14.25, 26; 16.12, 13
44 cf. Acts 1.1, 2; 2.43; 5.12
45 2 Cor. 12.12
46 Heb. 2.3, 4
47 2 Thess. 3.4, 6, 10, 12, 14
48 2 Cor. 13.3
49 Gal. 4.14
50 e.g. 3 Jn. 9
51 1 Jn. 4.6
52 see Eusebius'
   Ecclesiastical History
   III.xxxix, 15 and
   Irenaeus' *Adversus
   Haereses* III.1.i
53 Phil. 2.7
54 Mk. 13.32
55 e.g. Jn. 7.14–17; 12.49;
   17.8
56 Jn. 13.13

7. THE INTERPRETATION OF THE BIBLE

I once heard Dr. Alan Cole, of Sydney, remark that, surprising as it may seem, God sometimes blesses 'a poor exegesis of a bad translation of a doubtful reading of an obscure verse of a minor prophet'!

This is true. He does. But it gives us no possible excuse for slovenliness in Biblical interpretation. On the contrary, if the Bible is indeed God's word written, we should spare no pains and grudge no effort to discover what He has said (and says) in Scripture.

How then shall the student of the Bible grasp its message with accuracy? Where is he to look for help? Perhaps we should begin our answer by warning the reader against any pretension to infallibility. God's word is infallible, for what He has said is true. But no Christian individual, group or church has ever been or will ever be an infallible interpreter of God's word. Human interpretations belong to the sphere of tradition, and an appeal may always be made against tradition to the Scripture itself which tradition claims to interpret.

Nevertheless, God has made provision for us to grow in our understanding of the truth and to be protected from the worst forms of misinterpretation. He has given us three teachers to instruct us, and three principles to guide us.

The Enlightenment of the Holy Spirit

Our foremost teacher is the Holy Spirit Himself. 'Hermeneutics' is the technical name given to the science of interpreting Scripture, and it should be obvious that a truly Biblical hermeneutic will be consistent with the nature of the Bible itself. If, then, the Biblical authors spoke from God, not on their own impulse but as they were moved by the Holy Spirit,[1] it is the Holy Spirit who can interpret what He caused them to speak. The best interpreter of every book is its author, since He alone knows what He intended to say. So God's book can be interpreted by God's Spirit alone.

The work of the Holy Spirit in communicating God's truth to man is now seen to have two stages. The first and objective stage is 'revelation', the disclosure of the truth in Scripture. The second and subjective stage may be called 'illumination', the enlightenment of our minds to comprehend the truth disclosed in Scripture. Each process is indispensable. Without revelation we have no truth to perceive; without illumination no faculty with which to perceive it.

An illustration comes from the days of Isaiah when, in judgment upon His rebellious people, God ceased to speak to them. His truth became like a sealed book, and His people like illiterate children. There were thus two barriers to their receiving His word:

207

'When men give it to one who can read, saying "Read this", he says, "I cannot, for it is sealed". And when they give the book to one who cannot read, saying "Read this", he says, "I cannot read."' (Is. 29. 11, 12)

Once we grant the necessity of the Holy Spirit's illumination before we can understand God's word, we are ready to consider the kind of people the Holy Spirit enlightens.

First, the Holy Spirit enlightens the regenerate. An experience of rebirth is essential before we are able to grasp heavenly truth. 'Unless one is born anew', Jesus said, 'he cannot see the kingdom of God'.[3] This fact the apostle Paul echoed:

'The unspiritual man (the "natural" or "unregenerate" man) does not receive the gifts of the Spirit of God, for they are folly to him, and he is not able to understand them because they are spiritually discerned.'[4]

Many have borne witness to this out of their own experience. For example, William Grimshaw, one of the leading English evangelicals in the eighteenth century, said to a friend after his conversion that 'If God had drawn up His Bible to heaven, and sent him down another, it would not have been newer to him.'[5]

I can myself testify to something very similar. My mother brought me up to read a passage of the Bible every day. For her sake and out of habit I continued the practice until my later teens. But it was a largely meaningless routine, for I did not understand what I was reading. After my conversion, however, the Bible immediately began to become a living book to me. I am not of course claiming that I suddenly understood it all. Nor do I pretend that I no longer found some of it dull and difficult. But it assumed a new relevance for me, as the Holy Spirit illumined and applied its message to my life.

Secondly, the Holy Spirit enlightens the humble. There is no greater hindrance to understanding than pride, and no more essential condition than humility. Jesus put the matter beyond dispute:

'I thank Thee, Father, Lord of heaven and earth, that Thou hast hidden these things from the wise and understanding and revealed them to babes; yea, Father, for such was Thy gracious will.'[6]

The 'wise and understanding' from whom God hides himself are the intellectually proud, and 'babes' the humble and sincere. It is not the ignorance or even the simplicity of a child which Jesus commended, but its open, receptive and unprejudiced approach. It is to such only that God reveals Himself. As Charles Simeon wrote:

'In the beginning of my enquiries I said to myself, I am a fool; of that I am quite certain. One thing I know assuredly, that in religion of myself I know nothing. I do not therefore sit down to the perusal of Scripture in order to impose a sense on the inspired writers; but to receive one, as they give it me. I pretend not to teach them, I wish like a child to be taught by them.'[7]

There is only one way to express such an attitude of humble expectancy before God, and that is by prayer. We need both to pray before we read Scripture and to read it in a prayerful frame of mind, and many Christians have found it helpful to use some of the Bible's own prayers for illumination. For example, the Psalmist's petition:

'Open my eyes, that I may behold wondrous things out of thy law.'[8]

Or one of Paul's great prayers, in all of which he asks in some way for an increase of knowledge or understanding. For example:

'. . . That the God of our Lord Jesus Christ, the Father of glory, may give you a spirit of wisdom and of revelation in the knowledge of Him, having the eyes of your hearts enlightened, that you may know what is the hope to which He has called you, what are the riches of His glorious inheritance in the saints, and what is the immeasurable greatness of His power in us who believe . . .'.[9]

Such a humbling of ourselves before God, acknowledging our darkness and appealing for His enlightenment, will not go unrewarded. Not long after his conversion at Pembroke College, Oxford, George Whitefield wrote in his journal:

'I began to read the Holy Scriptures upon my knees, laying aside all other books, and praying over, if possible, every line and word. This proved meat indeed and drink indeed to my soul. I daily received fresh life, light and power from above.'[10]

Thirdly, the Holy Spirit enlightens the obedient. This is much emphasized. Since God's purpose through Scripture is not merely to 'instruct' in general terms but specifically 'to instruct you for salvation'.[11] He is concerned about the response which readers give to His word. And the degree of our responsiveness, of our willingness to hear and obey, will to a large extent determine the degree of understanding we receive. Thus Jesus promised that those who have a will to do God's will would know whether His teaching was true, and that He would show Himself personally to those who prove their love for Him by their obedience.[12] Conversely, it is those who violate their conscience by disobedience who make shipwreck of their faith.[13] Nobody who does not practise what he already knows can expect to advance in his knowledge.

Fourthly, the Holy Spirit enlightens the communicative. The understanding He gives us is not intended for our private enjoyment alone; it is given us to be shared with others. We hold it on trust. A lamp is not brought into a room to be put under a bed, Jesus said, but on a stand. In the same way He intended His teaching to be made known, not to be kept secret. The apostles were to take heed what and how they heard. They were to listen to their Master's teaching, in order to communicate it. Otherwise, they would not receive any more:

'The measure you give will be the measure you get, and still more will be given you.'[14]

The Christian's Disciplined Study

If the Holy Spirit is our first and foremost teacher, there is a sense in which we ourselves, in our very dependence on the Spirit, must also teach ourselves. That is to say, in the process of divine education we are not wholly passive, but are expected to use our own reason responsibly. For in our reading of Scripture divine illumination is no substitute for human endeavour. Nor is humility in seeking light from God alone inconsistent with the most disciplined industry in study.

Scripture itself lays great stress on the conscientious Christian use of the mind, not of course in order to stand in judgment on God's word, but rather in order to submit to it, to grapple with it, to understand it and to relate it to the contemporary scene. Indeed, there are frequent complaints in Scripture that man keeps forgetting his basic rationality as a human being made in God's image and behaves instead 'like a horse or a mule, without understanding'.[15]

So Jesus rebuked His apostles for their lack of understanding and their failure to use their common sense.[16] He reproached the multitudes similarly:

211

'Why do you not judge for yourselves what is right?'[17]

This command to 'judge for yourselves' is particularly prominent in Paul's first letter to Corinth. Here was a church which laid claim to great wisdom, but failed to exhibit it. Again and again Paul asks incredulously 'Do you not know. . . .?[18] and introduces his apostolic instruction with formulae like 'I want you to know, brethren' or 'I do not want you to be uninformed'.[19] He is clear that, whereas the natural or unregenerate man is unable to understand God's truth, the spiritual or regenerate man 'judges all things'. That is, what the natural man cannot discern, the spiritual man can and does, because he is inhabited and ruled by the Holy Spirit and so has 'the mind of Christ'.[20]

This conviction leads Paul, in this same Corinthian letter, to appeal to his readers' reason. He writes:

'I speak as to sensible men; judge for yourselves what I say'.[21]

In other New Testament letters similar exhortations occur. Christians are to 'test the spirits' (i.e. human teachers claiming divine inspiration) and indeed to 'test everything' they hear.[22] Again, when faced with difficult ethical decisions, they are to give their minds to the problem, so that each may be 'fully convinced in his own mind'.[23] It is a mark of Christian maturity to have our 'faculties trained by practice to distinguish good from evil.'[24]

We must, then, take seriously this Biblical injunction to use our rational and critical powers. We are not to oppose prayer and thought as alternative means of increasing our understanding of Scripture, but to combine them. Daniel in the Old Testament and Paul in the New are good examples of this balance:

'Fear not, Daniel, for from the first day that you set

your mind to understand and humbled yourself before
your God, your words have been heard. . . .'[25]

'Think over what I say, for the Lord will grant you
understanding in everything.'[26]

It is not enough to humble ourselves before God and
look to Him for understanding; we must also set our
minds to understand Scripture and think over what is
written in it. As Charles Simeon put it:

'For the attainment of divine knowledge, we are
directed to combine a dependence on God's Spirit
with our own researches. Let us, then, not presume to
separate what God has thus united.'[27]

Sometimes our growth in understanding is inhibited
by a proud and prayerless self-confidence, but at other
times by sheer laziness and indiscipline. He who would
increase in the knowledge of God must both abase himself before the Spirit of truth and commit himself to a
lifetime of study.

The Teaching of the Church

Our third teacher is the Church. So far our portrayal of
how God teaches His people from His word has been
entirely individualistic. And it has been true. For it is
God's loving purpose to enlighten, save, reform and
nourish His people by His word as each hears it or reads
it for himself. Our sixteenth-century reformers were quite
right to want to translate the Bible into plain English and
put it into the hands of plain people. For they were
appalled at the widespread ignorance of Scripture. Hence
William Tyndale's famous jibe to a clergyman critic:

'If God spare my life, ere many years pass I will cause a
boy that driveth the plough shall know more of the
Scriptures than thou dost.'[28]

We must also agree with the reformers' insistence on what they termed 'the right of private judgment', the birthright of every child of God to hear his Father's voice speaking to him directly through Scripture. This they asserted over against the claim of the Church of Rome that she had been given a unique 'magisterium' or teaching authority, because of which she alone could supply the true interpretation of Scripture.

Nevertheless, in rejecting every attempt to interpose the Church or any other authoritative teaching body between God and His people, we must not deny that the Church has a place in God's plan to give His people a right understanding of His word. The individual Christian's humble, prayerful, diligent and obedient study of Scripture is not the only way the Holy Spirit makes clear what He has revealed. It would hardly be humble to ignore what the Spirit may have shown to others. The Holy Spirit is indeed our teacher, but He teaches us indirectly through others as well as directly to our own minds. It was not to one man that He revealed the truths now enshrined in Scripture, but to a multiplicity of prophets and apostles; His work of illumination is given to many also. It is not as individuals merely, but 'with all the saints' that we are given 'power to comprehend . . . what is the breadth and length and height and depth, and to know the love of Christ which surpasses knowledge'.[29]

A recognition of this truth will give us more respect than we customarily have for 'tradition', that is, for the understanding of Biblical truth which has been handed down from the past to the present. Although the Holy Spirit's work of Biblical inspiration was unique, His teaching ministry did not cease when the last apostle died. It changed from revelation to illumination. Gradually and progressively over the centuries of Church history, the Spirit of truth enabled the Church to grasp, clarify and formulate the great doctrines of Scripture.

We owe much to the so-called Catholic Creeds ('catholic' because they were accepted by the whole Church) and Reformation confessions, together with the Biblical commentaries and theological treatises of individual scholars.

If we should not despise the heritage of the past, neither should we despise the teachers of the contemporary Church. The pastoral ministry is a teaching ministry, and 'pastors and teachers' are gifts which the ascended Christ still bestows upon His Church.[30] We should also be willing to listen to each other and learn from each other. The Holy Spirit can illumine our minds through group as well as individual Bible study. The apostle Paul clearly envisaged this kind of mutual instruction in the local church when he wrote:

'Let the word of Christ dwell in you richly, as you teach and admonish one another in all wisdom . . .'[31]

Luke gives a striking example of the role of the teacher in Acts 8.26–39. An Ethiopian minister of state, while travelling home from Jerusalem by chariot, was reading the prophecy of Isaiah. Philip the evangelist asked him: 'Do you understand what you are reading?' To which he replied: 'How can I, unless someone guides me?' So Philip went up to sit beside him and to explain the Scripture to him. Calvin comments:

'That is also why the reading of Scripture bears fruit with such a few people today, because scarcely one in a hundred is to be found who gladly submits himself to teaching. . . .

'Now if any of us is diffident about himself, but shows that he is teachable, angels will come down from heaven to teach us, rather than that the Lord allow us to labour in vain. However, following the example of the (Ethiopian) eunuch, we must make use of all the aids which the Lord sets before us for the understanding of Scripture. Fanatics seek inspirations from heaven, and at the same time despise the minister of God, by whose hand they ought to have been ruled. Others, relying on their own penetrating insight, do not deign to hear anybody or to read any commentaries. But God does not wish the aids, which He appoints for us, to be despised, and does not allow contempt of them to go unpunished. And we must keep in mind here, that not only is Scripture given to us, but interpreters and teachers are also added to help us. That is why the Lord chose Philip for the eunuch, rather than an angel'.[32]

Of course no human teacher is infallible, either of the past or of the present, and Christ forbade us to give any human teacher a slavish following.[33] Ultimately, God Himself is our teacher and, speaking ideally, we may all be described as 'taught by God'.[34] Indeed, in principle, because of the apostolic word and the anointing Spirit given to us all, we 'have no need that anyone should teach' us.[35] The right of private judgment must not be taken away from us. Sometimes it is even necessary for us, out of loyalty to the plain meaning of Scripture, to disagree with teachers in the Church and say (I hope humbly):

'I have more understanding than all my teachers, for Thy testimonies are my meditation'.[36]

Nevertheless, I must repeat that God has appointed teachers in His Church. It is our Christian duty to listen to them with respect, humility and eagerness, and to feed upon God's word from their lips when they faithfully expound it, at the same time ourselves 'examining the Scriptures daily' to see if what they say is true.[37]

Our three teachers, then, whom I have mentioned are the Holy Spirit, ourselves and the Church. It is by receiving the illumination of the Spirit, by using our own reason and by listening to the teaching of others in the Church that we grow in our understanding of Scripture. I am anxious not to be misunderstood. I am emphatically not saying that Scripture, reason and tradition are a threefold authority of equal importance by which we come to know God's truth. No. Scripture alone is God's word written, and the Holy Spirit its ultimate interpreter. The place of the individual's reason and of the Church's tradition lies in the elucidation and application of Scripture. But both are subordinate to God Himself as He speaks to us through His word.

We turn now from the three teachers who instruct us to the three principles which are to guide us in our interpretation of Scripture.

It is often said by our critics, especially by those who know what a high view of Scripture we take, that 'you can make the Bible mean anything you like'. They are probably thinking of non-Christian and semi-Christian cults which support their particular opinions by an arbitrary selection and interpretation of proof texts. But the New Testament itself condemns those who 'tamper with God's word' and 'twist' it to suit their own purposes.[38] To those who accuse us of this, I always reply: 'You are quite right. You *can* make the Bible mean anything you like—if you are unscrupulous enough. But if you are scrupulously honest in your approach to the Bible and in your use of sound principles of interpretation, far from your being able to manipulate Scripture, you will find Scripture controlling and directing you'. What, then, are these sound principles of interpretation?

The Natural Sense

First, we must look for the *natural* sense. I will call this the principle of simplicity.

217

One of our basic Christian convictions is that 'God is light and in Him is no darkness at all.'[39] That is to say, it is as much the nature of God to reveal Himself as it is the nature of light to shine. Now God has revealed Himself chiefly by speaking. We may be quite sure, therefore, that He has spoken in order to be understood, and that He has intended Scripture (the record of the divine speech) to be plain to its readers. For the whole purpose of revelation is clarity not confusion, a readily intelligible message, not a set of dark and mysterious riddles.

This principle of simplicity strikes at the root of much popular interpretation. For example, the destructive criticism of radical Christians would limit the truth to a tiny minority of scholars who claim the competence to sift the wheat from the chaff in Scripture, while the fanciful reconstructions of some evangelical Christians would turn Scripture into a complicated jigsaw puzzle to which they alone possess the key. Over against these distortions we must assert that God's whole purpose in speaking and in causing His speech to be preserved is that He wanted to communicate to ordinary people and save them.

It is true that in some matters Scripture is not as plain as in others. This is apparent from the fact that, although devout and careful students of the Bible, deeply concerned to submit to its authority, enjoy a very wide measure of agreement on the great fundamentals of historic Christianity, they still disagree on some points. One thinks, for example, of such questions as these: whether baptism should be administered only to adult believers or to the children of Christian parents as well, and whether candidates should be immersed in the water or have it poured over them; whether our doctrine of the church should be 'independent' (each local church being autonomous) or 'connexional' (local churches being in some way federated); whether the ministry of the church should be episcopal or presbyterian, or indeed whether the local assembly should rather have a non-professional pastoral oversight; whether miracles (e.g. the instantaneous healing of organic diseases without medical means) should be expected in the contemporary church regularly, occasionally or never; and whether the 'millenium' (the reign of Christ for a thousand years) is intended to be understood literally as a future earthly event or symbolically as a present spiritual reality.

When equally Biblical Christians disagree in such matters, what should we do? We should be humble enough to re-examine them ourselves in the light of sound principles of interpretation. And we should be mature enough to discuss them with one another without rancour. If then we still disagree, we must regard such disputed points as being secondary in importance and respect one another with mutual Christian love and tolerance. We should also rejoice that in all the central doctrines of the faith we remain agreed, for in these the Scripture is plain, perspicuous and virtually self-interpreting.

God chose human language as the vehicle of His self-revelation. In speaking to men through men He used the language of men. As a result, although Scripture is unlike all other books in being the word of God, it is also like all other books in being the words of men. Since it is unique because divine, we must study it like no other book, praying to the Holy Spirit for illumination. Since it is ordinary because human, we must study it like every other book, paying attention to the common rules of vocabulary, grammar and syntax. For if (as we saw in the previous chapter) God did no violence to the agents of His revelation (human persons), He did no violence to the instrument either (human language).

It follows that no serious Bible reader can escape the discipline of linguistic study. Best of all would be a knowledge of the original languages, Hebrew and Greek.

But most will read in English, and for them an accurate modern version is essential. Although popular paraphrases are useful additional helps, there is no substitute for a careful, scholarly translation like the Revised Version or the Revised Standard Version, which (though both revisions of the Authorised Version) are probably still the best translations available in English. To-day's English Version also deserves a special mention, since it combines reliability with unusually simple and straightforward language. An analytical Concordance (like Young's or Strong's) is another extremely valuable tool, for it not only groups the Biblical words according to the English (AV) text but then subdivides them into the original Hebrew and Greek words and gives their meaning.

In reading the words and sentences of the Biblical text, we must look first of all for their obvious and natural meaning. In Sir Charles Odgers' standard book on the interpretation of legal deeds and documents his third rule is that 'words are to be taken in their literal meaning'. Unless the subject-matter shows otherwise, he writes, 'the plain, ordinary meaning of the words used is to be adopted in construing a document'.[40]

Unfortunately, the fanciful allegorization of Scripture has often brought serious Bible reading into disrepute. It was already indulged in by Jewish commentators before Christ, of whom Philo of Alexandria was the notorious example. It is not surprising that some Christian commentators in the post-apostolic period tried their hand at the same game. The so-called *Epistle of Barnabas*, for instance, an apocryphal work of (probably) the early second century A.D., contains some outrageous allegorizations. In one passage the author quotes the Mosaic regulation that the Jews might eat every animal that divides the hoof and chews the cud, and explains it thus:

'Cleave unto those that fear the Lord, . . . with those who know that meditation is a work of gladness and who chew the cud of the word of the Lord. But why that which divides the hoof? Because the righteous man both walks in this world and at the same time looks for the holy world to come'.[41]

Now certainly to 'chew the cud' of God's word is a very suggestive expression for Bible meditation, and also the Christian is a citizen of two worlds. But equally certainly this is not what Moses had in mind when he wrote about cud-chewing, cloven-hoofed animals!

The allegorical school of interpretation was further promoted by Origen of Alexandria in the fourth century A.D. and by medieval churchmen. It is greatly to the credit of the sixteenth century reformers that they rescued Scripture from this kind of arbitrary treatment and insisted that what is simple and straightforward is always to be preferred to subtleties. John Calvin put it admirably:

'Let us know, then, that the true meaning of Scripture is the natural and obvious meaning; and let us embrace and abide by it resolutely. Let us not only neglect as doubtful, but boldly set aside as deadly corruptions, those pretended expositions which lead us away from the natural meaning'.[42]

To look for the natural meaning of Scripture is not necessarily the same as looking for the literal meaning. For sometimes the natural meaning is figurative rather than literal. Jesus Himself had to reproach some of His hearers for their excessive literalism. Nicodemus misunderstood His reference to a second birth so completely that he asked incredulously whether a man can re-enter his mother's womb and be born. The Samaritan woman seems to have supposed that the living, thirst-quenching water which He offered her was down Jacob's well. And when later Jesus claimed He could satisfy people's hunger by giving Himself to them as living bread, they asked 'how can this man give us His flesh to eat?'.[43] These examples should be enough to warn us against a dead and rigid literalism. It should have been obvious that Jesus was using figures of speech.

His favourite form of instruction was the parable, though occasionally He used the allegory. The difference between them is that in an allegory the similitude is drawn at many points, whereas the parable is an every-day story told to illustrate one main lesson, the wealth of detail being added not to teach subsidiary lessons but for dramatic effect. Examples of the allegory are the Good Shepherd in John 10, the Vine and the Branches in John 15 and the Sower in Mark 4. An example of the parable is the Good Samaritan.[44] Jesus told it in answer to the question 'Who is my neighbour?' and taught from it that true neighbour-love transcends the barriers of race and religion. It is not legitimate to press the details, e.g. to suggest that the inn represents the church and the two denarii given to the innkeeper the two sacraments. This would be to turn an obvious parable into an allegory and to provoke questions about what is represented by the brigands, the oil, the wine and the donkey!

Scripture is very rich in metaphorical language, and in every metaphor it is essential to ask at what point the analogy is being drawn. We must avoid arguing from analogy, that is, elaborating the correspondence beyond the limits which Scripture sets. Thus, God is our Father and we are His children. As our Father, He has begotten us, He loves us and cares for us. As His children, we depend on Him and must love and obey Him. But we have no liberty to argue, for example, that since God is our heavenly Father, we must also have a heavenly mother, on the ground that no child can have a father without a mother. Nor can we argue that because we are

222

called 'children', we can avoid the responsibility of adult thought and action. For the same Scripture which commends to us the humility of a little child also condemns in us a child's immaturity.

If some Scripture is literal and some figurative, how are we to tell which is which? The fundamental answer is that we are to look for the natural sense. Common sense will usually guide us. In particular, it is wise to ask ourselves what is the intention of the author or speaker. Let me give two examples.

First, it is often said that the Old Testament authors conceived the universe as a 'three-decker' construction with earth as man's dwelling-place, heaven above him like a great canopy punctured with holes through which the stars peeped, and *sheol* (the abode of the dead) beneath him; that they believed this in a literal and spatial way; and that when it rained, for instance, God had literally 'opened the windows of heaven'. I do not of course deny that this is the kind of language they used, but I do seriously doubt whether they believed it literally or intended their readers to understand it literally. Take Psalm 75. In verse 3 God is represented as saying that 'when the earth totters', it is He who 'keeps steady its pillars'. Did the psalmist think that the earth was literally balanced on stilts? I think not. In the next verse God commands the wicked 'do not lift up your horn' (a symbol of prosperity and success) and in verse 10 it is written that 'the horns of the wicked will be cut off', while in verse 8 we are told that in the Lord's hand 'there is a cup with foaming wine well mixed' (a symbol of His wrath). To me it is quite gratuitous to insist that the author thought the earth was set on literal pillars, unless we are prepared equally to insist that he thought the wicked have literal horns (which will one day be cut off) and that God holds a literal cup of foaming wine which He will one day pour out upon all the wicked of the earth.

My other example is taken from the special form of Biblical literature called 'apocalyptic', which claims to set forth hidden truths of both present reality and future history, usually in a series of weird and wonderful images. The Book of Revelation is a Christian apocalypse. In it God's redeemed people, gathered round His throne, are said to be wearing white robes which they have 'washed . . . and made . . . white in the blood of the Lamb'.[45] Now to take this literally would be rather repulsive. It would also be impossible, since robes laundered in lamb's blood would not come out white. No. The author clearly intends the expression as a symbol to be interpreted, not as an image to be visualized. We are to understand that the righteousness of God's people (their 'white robes') is due entirely to the death of Christ ('the blood of the Lamb') in which they have put their trust ('washed their robes'). Thus, in this case too, the 'natural' sense is the figurative, not the literal.

The Original Sense

Secondly, we must look for the *original* sense of Scripture. This is the principle of history.

We have seen in earlier chapters that God chose to reveal Himself in a precise historical context. Although His self-revelation is addressed to every man of every age and every country, each part of it was addressed in the first instance to a particular people of a particular age in a particular country. Therefore the permanent and universal message of Scripture can be understood only in the light of the circumstances in which it was originally given. It would obviously be very misleading to read back into Scripture the notions of a later age. As Charles Simeon wrote about the ideals of his preaching ministry:

'My endeavour is *to bring out of Scripture what is there, and not to thrust in what I think might be there. I*

224

have a great jealousy on this head; never to speak more
or less than I believe the mind of the Spirit, in the
passage I am expounding'.[46]

So, as we read the Bible, we need to keep asking ourselves: what did the author intend to convey by this?
What is he actually asserting? What will his original
hearers have understood him to have meant? This enquiry is commonly known as the 'grammatico-historical'
method of interpretation. J. Gresham Machen has described it well:

'Scientific historical method in the interpretation of the
Bible requires that the Biblical writers should be
allowed to speak for themselves. A generation or so
ago that feature of scientific method was exalted to the
dignity of a principle, and was honoured by a long
name. It was called "grammatico-historical exegesis".
The fundamental notion of it was that the modern
student should distinguish sharply between what he
would have said or what he would have liked to have
the Biblical writer say, and what the writer actually did
say'.[47]

As we attempt to transport ourselves back into the
author's mind and times, and to listen to his words as if
we were among his first readers, we shall need particularly to consider the situation, the style and the language
in which he wrote.

First, the situation. The proper function of literary and
historical criticism is to reconstruct the *mise en scène* of
the Biblical book in question. Who wrote it and to whom?
In what circumstances? For what reason? Floods of
light are thrown on the text of the Old Testament prophets, for example, if we can fit them into the story of
Israel. The same is true of the New Testament epistles and
the story of the early Church as Luke tells it in the Acts,

and specially the missionary journeys of Paul. For example, Paul's *Letter to the Philippians* becomes a much more human document if on the one hand we can picture the author under house arrest in Rome (or possibly Ephesus) and on the other Lydia, the jailor and the slave-girl (whose conversions are described in Acts 16) as among its first readers.

A careful consideration of the historical background to the letters of Paul and James would have protected Luther from finding them contradictory and from rejecting James' letter as made of 'straw'. It is true that Paul declared a man 'justified by faith apart from works of law' and gave Abraham as an example,[48] whereas James declared a man 'justified by works and not by faith alone' and also quoted Abraham as an example.[49] But their positions are not mutually irreconcilable. Paul was tilting at legalists who believed in salvation by works, James at religionists who believed in salvation by orthodoxy. Both believed that salvation was by faith and that a saving faith would manifest itself in good works. It was natural in their particular circumstances, however, that Paul should stress the faith which issues in works, and James the works which spring from faith.

Secondly, the style. It is important to take note of the literary *genre* of each Biblical book. Is it prose or poetry, historical narrative or wisdom literature? Is it law, prophecy, psalm or apocalyptic? Is it a drama, or a letter, or that distinctively Christian form called a 'gospel', a collection of the words and deeds of Jesus which bear witness to Him? How we interpret what we read, not least whether we take it literally or figuratively, will depend largely on its form and style.

Thirdly, the language. All human language is a living, changing thing. The meaning of words alters from century to century and culture to culture. We cannot read the word 'love' in Scripture and immediately suppose we know what it means. Four different Greek words are used in the New Testament, all translated 'love' in English. But each has a distinctive meaning, and only one expresses what Christians mean by love, which is poles apart from the erotica of twentieth-century glossy magazines.

For many centuries scholars were not able to recognize the kind of Greek in which the New Testament was written. It was neither classical Greek nor modern Greek. Some thought it was made up specially for the purpose. They even called it 'the language of the Holy Ghost'. But towards the close of the last century, in the dry sands of Egypt, archaeologists began to discover large quantities of ancient papyrus rolls. They were mostly secular and non-literary documents. Many had come from the waste paper baskets of public record offices, whose contents had been dumped on the local rubbish heap. And their Greek (the *koinē* or common language of every day) was found to be largely the same as that of the New Testament. So now the meaning of New Testament Greek words has to be sought against a background not only of classical Greek and of Hebrew thought but also of the secular language of the day. I will give one example only.

In his two letters to the Thessalonians Paul several times refers to those he describes as *ataktos*. In classical Greek the word was commonly used of soldiers who broke rank, of an army in disarray. So the Authorized Version translates the word 'disorderly', and it was assumed that there was an undisciplined group of some kind in the Thessalonian church. But two or three apprenticeship contracts were discovered among the papyri which contain an undertaking that should the boy play truant from work or exceed his annual holiday, the lost time would be made good. And the word for playing truant is *ataktos*, or rather its cognate verb. So the Revised Standard Version renders it not 'disorderly' but 'idle'. It seems probable that some Thessalonian Christians, believing that the Lord's return was imminent, were playing truant from work. It is these idle Christians whom Paul commands to mind their own affairs, work with their own hands and earn their own living, adding that 'if anyone will not work, let him not eat'.[50]

Before we leave this second principle of Biblical interpretation, another matter must be broached. Since God's revelation was given in a particular historical and geographical situation, this means that it had a particular cultural setting as well. And the social customs which form the background of some Biblical instruction are entirely foreign to those of our day. Are we then to reject the teaching because it is culturally dated? Or are we to go to the other extreme and try to invest both teaching and setting with the same permanent validity? Neither of these seems to be the right way to escape the dilemma. The third and better way is to accept the Biblical instruction itself as permanently binding, but to translate it into contemporary cultural terms. Thus, Jesus commanded His disciples to wash one another's feet as a mark of the mutual love which humbles itself to serve, and the apostles Paul and Peter commanded their readers, when they came together, to greet one another with a holy kiss or a kiss of love.[51] We have no liberty to repudiate these commandments. But nor should we give them a slavishly literal obedience. For nowadays (at least in the west) we do not walk through dusty streets in sandals, and therefore do not need to have our feet washed. Nor is it customary to go round kissing everybody in public. Nevertheless, we can and must obey Christ's injunction through other outward forms of humble service, and obey the apostles' command by 'a handshake all round', as J. B. Phillips aptly paraphrases the kiss of peace. Let it be clear that the purpose of such a cultural transposition is not to avoid obedience, but rather to ensure it.

A more difficult example of the tension between the permanently valid and the culturally dated concerns the status, behaviour and dress of women. Are we to retain all the detailed Biblical requirements, or—in deference to the increasingly vocal 'Women's Lib' movement—jettison the lot? Again there seems to be a wiser middle course. Consider the question of the veiling of women, to which Paul devotes half a chapter in First Corinthians (11). He insists that it is dishonourable, even disgraceful, for a woman to pray or prophesy in public with her head unveiled. He appeals to reason, nature, ecclesiastical custom and his own apostolic authority in support of his teaching. What are we to make of this? Perhaps the commonest and most superficial reaction is to suppose that the apostle's requirement is met if women wear hats in church. But eastern veils and western hats are entirely different, theologically as well as culturally! One of the crucial statements of Paul's argument occurs in verse 10 where, in referring to a woman's duty 'to have a veil on her head' (RSV), he actually writes that she ought to wear 'authority' (RSV margin) on her head. This is the point. In those days the veil the woman wore was a symbol of her husband's authority over her. Not only does a woman's hat not have this significance today, but some modern modes appear to symbolize the exact reverse—liberation, not submission! What is permanently valid in Paul's teaching is the authority of the husband, for he grounds it on unchanging theological truths concerning creation. What is culturally dated is the veil. We must find other social customs which express a woman's acceptance of the authority which God has given to man.

In addition, we must be very careful how we interpret the husband's 'authority'. The word is by no means a synonym for authoritarianism. Nor can it be taken to express any 'superiority' of the male or 'inferiority' of the female. For—centuries in advance of his time—Paul emphatically declared that in Christ 'there is neither male nor female'.[52] He also drew a profound analogy between the relationship of husband and wife in marriage and the relationship between the Father and the Son in the Godhead.[53] This suggests that the husband's 'headship' over his wife is not incompatible with their equality, any more than is the Father's 'headship' over Christ. Perhaps the husband's authority should be understood in terms rather of responsibility than of autocracy, the responsibility of a loving care.

The General Sense

Thirdly, we must look for the *general* sense of Scripture. This is the principle of harmony.

From a human standpoint the Bible is a symposium with a wide assortment of contributors. From the divine standpoint, however, the whole Bible emanates from one mind. It is the word of God expressing the mind of God, and so possesses an organic unity. For this reason we must approach Scripture with the confidence both that God has spoken and that, in speaking, He has not contradicted Himself.

Sir Charles Odgers, in the book mentioned earlier, gives as his seventh rule for interpreting legal documents 'the deed is to be construed as a whole'. He goes on:

'The deed must be read and interpreted as a whole in order to extract the meaning of any particular part or expression . . . Every part of the deed ought to be compared with the other and one entire sense ought to be made thereof . . . Every part of it may be brought into action in order to collect from the whole one uniform and consistent sense, if that may be done. . . .

The words of each clause should be so interpreted as to bring them into harmony with the other provisions of the deed if that interpretation does no violence to the meaning of which they are naturally susceptible'.[54]

As with legal documents, so with the Biblical text we should seek to resolve apparent discrepancies and interpret Scripture as one harmonious whole. This will lead us to interpret Scripture by Scripture, especially what is obscure by what is plain, and never so to 'expound one place of Scripture that it be repugnant to another'.[55]

This was John Knox's argument with Mary Queen of Scots. In a private debate with her in Edinburgh in 1561 he asserted that the Church of Rome (which she said she would defend as the true Church of God) had declined from the purity of religion taught by the apostles. The Queen herself, he added, possessed little right knowledge, since she had heard no teachers but those allowed by the Pope and his Cardinals. At this the Queen said:

'Ye interpret the Scriptures in one manner, and they in another; whom shall I believe, and who shall judge?'

John Knox replied:

'Believe God, that plainly speaketh in His Word: And further than the Word teacheth you, ye shall neither believe the one nor the other. The Word of God is plain in itself; And if there appear any obscurity in one place, the Holy Ghost, which is never contrarious to Himself, explains the same more clearly in other places'.[56]

We may say, therefore, that every text of Scripture has a double context, historical and scriptural. Its context in history is the situation in which it was written. Its context in Scripture is the place where it is found. So each text must be understood against both its historical and its scriptural background. These are our second and third principles of interpretation respectively, the principles of history and of harmony.

Further, the scriptural context of every text is both immediate (the paragraph, chapter and book in which it is embedded) and distant (the total Biblical revelation).

The immediate context is the more obvious. To wrench a text from its context is an inexcusable blunder, and many horrific tales are told of preachers who have done it. In his instruction on the local church's responsibility to discipline an impenitent offender, Jesus said: 'if he refuses to hear the church, let him be to you as a Gentile . . .' i.e. let him be excommunicated.[57] Now during the Tractarian movement which sought to restore the Church of England's 'catholic' authority, its followers preached so often on the three words of this verse 'hear the church' that they provoked Archbishop Whately to retort with a sermon on the equally truncated text 'if he refuses to hear the church, let him . . .'!

Perhaps this kind of trickery, which exploits a combination of words without any respect for their true contextual meaning, is so outrageous as to be comparatively rare. Yet I was myself greatly disturbed that the World Council of Churches (which ought to have known better) should take as the text for their Fourth Assembly at Uppsala in 1967 God's great words in Revelation 21.5 'Behold, I make all things new', where the sentence applies to what He is going to do in the end when He makes a new heaven and a new earth, and should then proceed without any conceivable justification to apply it to the political, revolutionary movements of today.

It is in some ways even more important that we should learn to see the Bible as a whole, and to read each text in the light of all. Let me give some examples of what I mean.

I promised in Chapter 3 that I would say something

232

more about the early chapters of Genesis. Perhaps these chapters are specially susceptible to misunderstanding whenever they are isolated from the rest of Scripture. My own position is to accept the historicity of Adam and Eve, but to remain agnostic about some details of the story like the precise nature of the tree of life and of the serpent. This is not to be arbitrary or inconsistent, however, for I have Biblical reasons for both. That Adam and Eve were literal people seems clear from Romans 5.12–21, where Paul draws a deliberate contrast between the disobedience of Adam through which sin and death entered the world and the obedience of Christ who secured salvation and life. The analogy is meaningless if Adam's act of disobedience was not an event as historical as Christ's act of obedience. But as for the serpent and the tree of life, they both reappear in the *Book of Revelation*, where they are clearly symbolical, the serpent representing Satan and the tree eternal life. So I have a *Biblical* (New Testament) reason for believing that Adam and Eve were historical, and an equally *Biblical* reason for supposing that the serpent and the trees in the story may in some sense be meant to be figurative.

When I was a Cambridge undergraduate, I can remember being rather perplexed by the verse which says that the ten commandments were written on stone tablets by the finger of God.[58] Was I required to believe this literally? Did a divine finger really appear and somehow inscribe Hebrew letters on stone? Certainly it is not impossible, for 'the fingers of a man's hand appeared and wrote on the plaster of the wall of the king's palace' in the case of King Belshazzar, announcing his imminent doom.[59] But today I am not so sure that we were ever meant to take literally the statement about the finger of God writing the law. For now I have read the Bible more thoroughly, and I have come across other references to God's fingers, all of which are symbolical. Thus, David referred to the heavens as the work of God's fingers.[60] Again, after the plague of gnats on man and beast the Egyptian magicians said to Pharaoh 'This is the finger of God', and after Jesus had begun to cast out demons He claimed to do it 'by the finger of God'.[61] If then, the reference to God's finger in the writing of the law is comparable to these other references, it seems that 'the finger of God' is a Biblical figure of speech for God's immediate intervention whether in creation (the heavens), in revelation (the law), in judgment (the plagues) or in salvation (the exorcism of demons). Such an interpretation would be in keeping with the principle of harmony.

Another example of the importance of considering each part of Scripture's teaching on any subject in the light of the whole is the second coming of Christ. It would be easy (and dangerous) to be selective in the texts from which we build up our doctrine. Thus, some passages indicate that Christ's return will be personal and visible, indeed that He will come 'in the same way' as He went.[62] But before we press this into meaning that the Return will be a kind of Ascension in reverse, like a film played backwards, and that Christ will set His feet on the precise spot on the Mount of Olives from which He was taken up, we need to consider something Jesus said to counter those who wanted to localize His return:

'As the lightning flashes and lights up the sky from one side to the other, so will the Son of man be in His day'.[63]

The truly Biblical Christian, anxious to be faithful to all Scripture, will want to do equal justice to both these strands of teaching. The coming of the Lord will indeed be personal, historical and visible; but it will also be 'in power and great glory', as universal as the lightning, a transcendent event of which the whole human population of both hemispheres will be simultaneously aware.

In my last examples of the need to see Scripture as a

whole, I want to say something about both the Mosaic law and the fulfilment of prophecy. This will throw light on the relation between the Old and the New Testaments, and so on the question of progressive revelation. The principle of harmony does not deny that there has been progression in God's revelation of Himself and of His purposes, but emphasizes rather that the progression has not been from error to truth, but from truth to more truth.

Take the law of Moses. It is recognised in both Old and New Testaments that Moses' law was God's law. Moses was but the intermediary through whom God gave His law to His people. But does the divine origin of the law mean that it is all still permanently binding on Christian people? No. For Moses' law was a complex code, consisting of moral instructions, ceremonial regulations and civil statutes. The New Testament clearly teaches that the *ceremonial* rules are now obsolete, the temple, priesthood and sacrifices having been fulfilled in Christ and the food laws having been abolished by Him.[64] The *civil* laws of Moses still have importance as indications of divine righteousness and justice, but no church or nation is under obligation to enact and enforce them today. There are several reasons for this. For one thing, the civil code of Moses was framed for a people who belonged to God by redemption; they were both a nation and a church simultaneously, whereas today no church is a nation and no nation a church. For another, it was adapted to an emergent nation, who were first a nomadic and then an agricultural community. The *moral* laws of Moses, however, have not been abrogated. On the contrary, they are still in force. Christ died that the righteous requirement of the law might be fulfilled in us, and the Holy Spirit writes God's law in our hearts.[65] Article VII of the Church of England's *Thirty-Nine Articles* sums up these distinctions well:

235

'Although the laws given from God by Moses, as touching ceremonies and rites, do not bind Christian men, nor the civil precepts thereof ought of necessity to be received in any commonwealth; yet notwithstanding, no Christian man whatsoever is free from the obedience of the commandments which are called moral.'

We turn now from law to prophecy. The great conviction of the New Testament authors is that with Jesus Christ the 'last days' foretold throughout the Old Testament had come, and that in Him and in His people the great promises of God found their fulfilment. Paul could even claim before King Agrippa:

'I stand here testifying both to small and great, saying nothing but what the prophets and Moses said would come to pass . . . .'.[66]

There is some disagreement among Biblical Christians as to whether we are to expect the Old Testament promises about Israel's future to be literally fulfilled, and whether the modern state of Israel in its occupation of the Holy Land is at least a partial fulfilment of them. Certainly God has a great future for the Jews, which is figuratively set forth by Paul as the grafting back into their own olive tree of the natural branches which had been broken off.[67] But there is no mention in the New Testament of any literal return of the Jews to the promised land. The overwhelming emphasis of the New Testament is that the Christian Church is now 'the Israel of God', 'the true circumcision', 'a chosen race, a royal priesthood, a holy nation, God's own people',[68] and that God's great promises to Abraham of both a posterity and a land are fulfilled spiritually in Christ and His Church:

'So you see that it is men of faith who are sons of

236

Abraham . . . Those who are men of faith are blessed with Abraham who had faith.'

'Christ redeemed us from the curse of the law, having become a curse for us . . . that in Christ Jesus the blessing of Abraham might come upon the Gentiles, that we might receive the promise of the Spirit through faith.'

'If you are Christ's, then you are Abraham's offspring, heirs according to promise.'[69]

To be more precise, the fulfilment of Old Testament prophecy is usually in three stages. First came an immediate or literal fulfilment. The second stage, in which we are living, is the gospel or spiritual fulfilment. One day will come the third stage, which will be the final or heavenly fulfilment. Thus, the promise to Abraham of an innumerable posterity was historically fulfilled in the children of Israel,[70] is being fulfilled today in Christ's people, and will be consummated in heaven in the 'great multitude which no man could number' round God's throne.[71] Or again, the Old Testament prophets predicted the rebuilding of the temple, and there was an immediate and literal rebuilding under Zerubbabel. Today, however, it is the Christian Church which is 'a holy temple in the Lord, . . . a dwelling place of God in the Spirit',[72] and so is the individual Christian's body also.[73] In the new or heavenly Jerusalem, however, there will be no separate temple, 'for its temple is the Lord God the Almighty and the Lamb' dwelling in the midst of His people for evermore.[74]

*　　*　　*

In conclusion, let me emphasize that the three principles of Biblical interpretation we have been considering are not arbitrary. They are derived from the character of the Bible itself as God's word written.

We look for the *natural* meaning because we believe

that God intended His revelation to be a plain and readily intelligible communication to ordinary human beings.

We look for the *original* meaning because we believe that God addressed His word to those who first heard it, and that it can be received by subsequent generations only in so far as they understand it historically. Our understanding may be fuller than that of the first hearers (e.g. of the prophecies of Christ); it cannot be substantially different.

We look for the *general* meaning because we believe that God is self-consistent, and that His revelation is self-consistent also.

So our three principles (of simplicity, history and harmony) arise partly from the nature of God and partly from the nature of Scripture as a plain, historical, consistent communication from God to men. They lay upon us a solemn responsibility to make our treatment of Scripture coincide with our view of it.

For Further Reading

Understanding God's Word by the Rev. Alan M. Stibbs (IVF 1950, 64 pages). The author was a gifted Bible expositor and for many years Vice-Principal of Oak Hill Theological College, London. He lists the rules—both 'general' and 'special'—for interpreting the text of Scripture. A wise, balanced and suggestive little book.

A Christian's Guide to Bible Study by A. Morgan Derham (Hodder & Stoughton 1963, 63 pages). The author writes from the conviction 'that straightforward Bible study is possible for the ordinary Christian', and indeed as exciting as it is neglected. After some introductory material on the Bible's authority and purpose, he lists six 'Basic Principles' to guide the reader in his interpretation, and goes on to give practical suggestions on both methods of study (with some concrete examples) and the necessary tools.

Principles of Biblical Interpretation by Louis Berkhof (Baker Book House 1950, 169 pages). A rather technical but very thorough treatment by the former President of Calvin Seminary, Grand Rapids. After introductory chapters on the history of interpretation among the Jews and in the Church, and on the inspiration, unity, diversity and style of Scripture, the author elaborates three basic principles of interpretation – grammatical, historical and theological. A textbook for preachers and teachers.

NOTES

1 2 Pet. 1.21
2 Is. 29.11, 12
3 Jn. 3.3
4 1 Cor. 2.14
5 *Five Christian Leaders of the Eighteenth Century* by Bishop J. C. Ryle, first published 1868. Banner of Truth edition 1960 p. 28
6 Mt. 11.25, 26
7 J. J. Gurney's memoir of an afternoon spent in Cambridge with Simeon in 1831, recorded in *Memoirs of the Life of the Rev. Charles Simeon* edited by William Carus (Hatchard 1847) p. 674
8 Ps. 119.18
9 Eph. 1.17–19 cf. 3.14–19; Phil. 1.9–11 and Col. 1.9–14
10 *George Whitefield's Journals*, first published between 1738 and 1741.

Banner of Truth edition 1960, p. 60
11 2 Tim. 3.15
12 Jn. 7.17; 14.21
13 1 Tim. 1.19
14 Mk. 4.21–25
15 Ps. 32.9
16 e.g. Mk. 8.17–21
17 Lk. 12.57
18 1 Cor. 3.16; 5.6; 6.2, 3, 9, 15, 16, 19
19 e.g 1 Cor. 10.1; 12.1
20 1 Cor. 2.14–16
21 1 Cor. 10.15 cf. 11.13
22 1 Jn. 4.1
23 Rom. 14.5
24 Heb. 5.14
25 Dan. 10.12
26 2 Tim. 2.7
27 sermon 975 in *Horae Homileticae.* 1819
28 Recorded in Foxe's *Book of Martyrs* Vol. IV
29 Eph. 3.18, 19
30 Eph. 4.11, 12
31 Col. 3.16

32 Commentary on Acts
   8.31 in the Oliver and
   Boyd edition p. 247
33 Mt. 23.8–10
34 Is. 54.13; Jn. 6.45; 1
   Thess. 1.9
35 1 Jn. 2.15–27
36 Ps. 119.99
37 Acts 17.11
38 2 Cor. 4.2; 2 Pet. 3.16
39 1 Jn. 1.5
40 *The Construction of
   Deeds and Statutes*.
   First published by Sweet
   and Maxwell in 1939.
   Fourth Edition 1956 p.27
41 *The Apostolic Fathers*
   edited by J. B. Lightfoot.
   Macmillan 1891 p. 279
42 Comment on Galatians
   4.22. William Pringle's
   translation (Calvin
   Translation Society)
   1854 p. 136
43 Jn. 3.3, 4; 4.10–15; 6.51,
   52
44 Lk. 10.29–37
45 Rev. 7.14
46 The italics are Simeon's.
   The quotation comes
   from a letter to his
   publisher Mr. Holdsworth
   (undated, although
   apparently 1832) in
   *Memoirs of the Life of
   the Rev. Charles Simeon*
   (edited by William Carus.
   Hatchard 1847 2nd
   edition p. 703)
47 *What is Faith?* by J.
   Gresham Machen 1st
   published 1925. Hodder
   edition (undated) p. 24
48 Rom. 3.28; 4.1–3
49 Jas. 2.21–24
50 1 Thess. 4.11; 5.14; 2
   Thess. 3.6–12
51 Jn. 13.12–17; Rom.
   16.16; 2 Cor. 13.12; 1
   Thess. 5.26; 1 Pet. 5.14
52 Gal. 3.28
53 1 Cor. 11.3
54 *ibid*. p. 39
55 Article XX *Of the
   Authority of the Church*
   from the Church of
   England's Thirty-nine
   Articles
56 The debate is recorded
   near the beginning of
   Book 4 of *The History
   of the Reformation of the
   Church of Scotland* by
   John Knox. Unfinished
   edition 1587. 1st
   complete edition 1644
   p. 314
57 Mt. 18.17
58 Ex. 31.18; Deut. 9.10
59 Dan. 5.5, 24–28
60 Ps. 8.3
61 Ex. 8.19; Lk. 11.20
62 Acts 1.11
63 Lk. 17.24 cf. Mt. 24.27
64 Consider the use of the
   words 'shadow' and
   'copy' in Heb. 8.5; 9.24;
   10.1 and Mark's
   editorial comment in
   7.19
65 Rom. 8.3, 4; Jer. 31.33
   cf. 2 Cor. 3.6–8
66 Acts 26.22
67 Rom. 11.13–27

68 Gal. 6.16; Phil. 3.3; 1
   Pet. 2.9
69 Gal. 3.7, 9, 13, 14, 29 cf.
   Rom. 4.13, 16. In verse
   13 God's promise to
   Abraham and his
   descendants is 'that they
   should inherit the
   world'. cf. 1 Cor. 3.21–23
70 cf. Num. 23.10; 1
   Kings 4.20
71 Rev. 7.9

72 Eph. 2.21, 22; cf. 1 Cor.
   3.16. Consider also how
   James saw in the
   Gentiles' inclusion in the
   Church a fulfilment of
   God's promise through
   Amos to rebuild the
   ruins of David's dwelling.
   Acts 15.13–18; Amos
   9.11, 12
73 1 Cor. 6.19, 20
74 Rev. 21.3, 22

8. THE USE OF THE BIBLE

Basic to our Christian faith is the conviction that our God, far from being dead and dumb, is living and vocal. He has spoken a precise message in a precise historical and geographical context, and has caused it to be written and preserved in the Bible. Moreover, as we have considered, there are sound reasons for accepting the Bible's authority and sound principles to guide us in its interpretation.

So what? Why have we spent so much time on these matters? For one reason only, that God still speaks through what He has spoken. What He said centuries ago has a vital relevance to contemporary men and women. The Bible is not an antique piece whose proper home is a museum. On the contrary, it is a 'lamp' to our feet and a 'light' to our path.[1] God's words can be our 'counsellors' in all the perplexities of modern life. They give wisdom and understanding to the simple.[2]

But whether we derive any benefit from Scripture depends on how we use it, on what response we make to its message. One of God's recurring complaints in the Biblical record itself is that His people continually turned a deaf ear to His word. His messengers had to keep pleading with Israel:

'O that today you would hearken to His voice!'³

There are in the end only two possible attitudes to God's word, to receive it or to reject it. Those who are receptive to it are portrayed with vivid figures of speech. They are said to 'tremble' at it, just because it is the word of the great God Himself.⁴ They prize it like gold and relish it like honey.⁵ They rejoice over it 'like one who finds great spoil'. They thirst for it with the ardour of a suckled child.⁶ On the other hand those who reject it are said to have closed their ears and refused to listen, 'stiffening their neck' and following 'the stubbornness of their evil heart'.⁷ Of such there is no more notorious example than King Jehoiakim, who, as the scroll of God's words through Jeremiah was read to him, first used a penknife to cut it into pieces and then threw the pieces into the fire until the whole scroll had been burned.⁸

Jesus similarly warned His contemporaries about their response to His teaching. In the Parable of the Sower the different soils into which the seed fell were intended to exemplify the varying reception which people give God's word. Jesus solemnly insisted that we shall be judged on the last day by the word He has spoken.⁹ All of us are building our life on some foundation. Those who build on rock, whose house will survive the storms of adversity and of judgment, are those who listen to Christ's teaching and put it into practice.¹⁰

To begin with, to listen involves time. Do we really believe that *God* has spoken, that *God's* words are recorded in Scripture, and that as we read it we may hear *God's* voice addressing us? Then we shall not grudge the time to listen. Instead, we shall want to register our protest against the rat-race of twentieth-century life and strive to recover the lost art of meditation. It is not a casual, superficial acquaintance with Scripture that the modern Church needs, but rather to heed our Master's exhortation:

'Let these words sink into your ears.'[11]

There is no particular secret about how to do it. It just takes time, purposefully redeemed from our busy lives, in which to turn Scripture over and over in our minds until it sinks into our hearts and so regulates everything we think and do. It is those who thus 'meditate day and night' in God's word whom He pronounces 'blessed'.[12]

If there is no single secret, there are no hard and fast rules either. For example, the practice of the daily 'Quiet Time' of Bible reading and prayer, preferably first thing in the morning and last thing at night, is not an inviolable tradition. It has certainly stood the test of time and brought untold profit to many generations of Christians. I am myself old-fashioned enough to retain confidence in it as an extremely valuable discipline. But it is still only a tradition; it has not been laid down in Scripture. So we have no liberty to add it to the decalogue as a kind of eleventh commandment. Nor was such a practice possible before the invention of printing and the availability of cheap Bibles for all. To insist on it as indispensable to Christian living would be to disqualify the millions of Christians who lived in the first fifteen centuries.

The great value of some Scripture meditation and prayer (however brief) at the beginning of each day is that it prepares us to bear the day's responsibilities and face the day's temptations. It seems unwise, to say the least, to go into the conflict unarmed. Nevertheless, the mother who has to cook the breakfast, and then get husband off to work and children off to school, may have to postpone her time with God until later in the morning, while the breadwinner who leaves home very early may prefer to requisition a little time from his (or her) lunch break.

However busy one's daily timetable may be, the increasing numbers who work a five-day week should be able to devote a longer time to Bible reading and prayer over the week-end. Sunday afternoon has obvious possibilities, or even Sunday evening since there is nothing in Scripture requiring Christians to attend church twice every Sunday! Further, if daily family prayers are impossible from Monday to Friday because work and school demand staggered meal-times, a weekly time when the family honours God together in their home, whatever form it takes, should be possible during the weekend.

It is not only by personal or family Bible reading that we can hear God's word, however. It is also through group Bible studies, whether organized by the local church or by a Christian Union or by ourselves in our own home, and (above all) through the public exposition of Scripture in church. I wish modern Christians took this more seriously. It is easy to blame the pulpit, but very often the pew gets the kind of pulpit ministry it wants. God said to Jeremiah:

'An appalling and horrible thing has happened in the land: the prophets prophesy falsely, and the priests rule at their direction; *My people love to have it so*. . . .'[13]

Congregations have far more responsibility than they commonly recognize for the kind of ministry they receive. They should encourage their minister to expound Scripture. They should come to church in a receptive and expectant mood, preferably bringing their Bible with them, hungry to hear what the Lord God may have to say to them through the lessons and the sermon. It may also be wise to take some steps to retain the message in their memory, perhaps by writing the text on a card and then

245

meditating on it during the rest of the week. And if the church we attend is not blessed with a ministry of Biblical exposition, the modern cassette recorder has brought the ministry of other Bible teachers within reach of many people, for personal or group listening.

Precisely how the individual Christian or the Christian family seeks to receive the message of the Bible is not the most important question. What is vital is that in some way at some time, and that regularly, we learn to listen to God's word and to feed upon it in our hearts.

This listening to God's voice in and through His word is only the beginning, however. It is not enough to 'know these things', Jesus said; we shall be blessed only if we 'do them'.[14] For according to the New Testament the truth is something to be 'done', not merely 'known'.[15] Perhaps no apostle put this more clearly than James, the Lord's brother, who wrote:

'But be doers of the word, and not hearers only, deceiving yourselves.'[16]

To 'do' the truth is to do what it says, to translate its message into action. This sounds simple, but it has far-reaching implications simply because the truth we have to 'do' is so rich. Let me give five facets of the life-style of a 'doer of the word'.

Worship

First, worship. Worship is impossible without a knowledge of the truth. I grant that Paul found an altar in Athens which was inscribed 'to an unknown God'. But it is ludicrous to try to worship a deity we do not know, for if we do not know Him we do not know what kind of worship He desires. Conversely, once we have even begun to know the living and true God, we must worship Him. And the more we come to know Him, the more we shall

246

realise that He is worthy of our devotion. For to worship is to praise God's name, to glory in who and what He is in the splendour of His being and His works:

'Let them praise the name of the Lord, for His name alone is exalted; His glory is above earth and heaven.'[17]

Since worship is always a response to the truth of God we perceive, it is supremely the word of God (His self-revelation) which evokes the worship of God. Therefore the Bible has an indispensable place in both public and private worship. In all public worship there should be a reading (or readings) of Scripture, and an exhortation or instruction based on it.[18] Far from being an intrusion into the service, both are essential to worship. So those who have the privilege of reading lessons in church should take pains to understand the passage, and those who are called to preach should be conscientious in studying both God's word and man's world in order to relate the one to the other. Only when God speaks through His word, making Himself known in the greatness of His glory and grace, do the congregation truly bow down and worship.

The same principle applies to private devotion. Apart from a humble prayer for illumination, we should worship and pray *after* our Bible reading. For it is from Scripture that we shall learn whom to worship and how to pray according to God's will.[19]

Repentance and Faith

The second mark of a 'doer of the word' is repentance. For God's word tells us what *we* are as well as what *He* is, discloses to us our sin, and calls us to confess and forsake it. Several of the graphic similes of Scripture enforce this truth. The word of God is like a mirror, showing us what we are like,[20] like a sword to prick our guilty conscience,[21] and like both a hammer and a fire to

247

break and purify us.[22] Whenever we read the Scripture we hear God saying to us:

> 'Thus says the Lord of hosts. . . . "Amend your ways and your doings. . . . Remove the evil of your doings from before My eyes; cease to do evil, learn to do good. . . ." '[23]

The third characteristic of the 'doer of the word' is faith. Faith is an integral part of the Christian life, for 'without faith it is impossible to please' God.[24] Christians are frequently described in the New Testament as 'believers' who 'through faith and patience inherit the promises'.[25] But faith is very commonly misunderstood. It is not screwing ourselves up to believe something which we strongly suspect is not true; it is resting confidently on Him who is true. Faith cannot exist in a vacuum or in isolation; it is always a trustful response to a trustworthy person. We must never set faith and knowledge over against one another as if they were mutually exclusive. For faith is based on knowledge:

> 'Those who know Thy name put their trust in Thee.'[26]

We trust God because we know Him to be trustworthy. How? Because He has revealed Himself to be such. As we read in Scripture about the character and mighty deeds of God, about His faithfulness to His covenant in the history of Israel, about 'His precious and very great promises',[27] about Jesus Christ in whom all God's promises find their 'yes',[28] and about the men of faith who were 'fully convinced that God was able to do what He had promised',[29] our faith is quickened, nourished and matured.

So then it is no use moaning that we seem to suffer from a chronic unbelief, or envying others ('I wish I had your faith'), as if our lack of faith were like our temperament, a congenital condition which cannot be changed.

For God himself has given us the means to increase our faith:

'Faith comes from what is heard, and what is heard comes by the preaching of Christ.'[30]

We have to take time and trouble to hear in order to believe. The Christian who wants to grow in faith must spend time meditating on God's word. He will soon discover what is meant by 'the encouragement of the Scriptures'.[31]

Obedience

Obedience is the fourth way by which we become 'doers' of the word and not only 'hearers'. Yet obedience involves submission to authority, and this is out of fashion today. However, if Jesus Christ Himself lived in humble obedience to God's word, obeying its commands as well as believing its promises, there can be no doubt that we must also. For the servant is not greater than his master.

Jesus went further than that. He indicated that, just as ancient Israel was to prove her love for God by obeying Him, so Christian disciples must prove their love for Christ by their obedience:

'If you love Me, you will keep my commandments . . . He who has My commandments and keeps them, he it is who loves Me . . . If a man loves Me, he will keep My word . . . he who does not love Me does not keep My words'.[32]

It seems to me that we should be more grateful to God than we customarily are that He has revealed His will so clearly on so many subjects in His word. For the very first step towards holiness of life is a knowledge of what is pleasing and displeasing to God.[33] So the Christian's dearest ambition is 'to live according to Scripture',[34] for there is no other way to be sure of living according to His will.

This goes for social as well as personal righteousness. For the will of God in the word of God for the people of God relates to the whole of our lives. It tells us to love God, to control ourselves and to love and serve our neighbour. And the requirement of neighbour-love has many and wide ramifications. For my neighbour has a body as well as a soul, and lives by God's ordering in a community. So I cannot claim to love him if I ignore either his physical or his social well-being.

We have already seen with what detailed applications the Hebrew prophets proclaimed the righteousness of God. The home, the market place, the law-court, the farm—these were the places where righteousness was to be practised. And where it was lacking, there the judgment of God would fall. The prophets were fearless in thundering their woes upon the unrighteous, upon the trader who cheated his customers by using false weights and measures, upon the greedy landowner who joined house to house and field to field until there was no more room, upon the magistrate who perverted justice by taking bribes from the guilty rich and condemning the innocent poor, upon the husband who profaned the divine institutions of marriage and home by his sexual unfaithfulness, upon the moneylender who charged extortionate rates of interest, even upon the king who oppressed the people instead of serving them. And by contrast the Book of Proverbs, full of practical wisdom, extols the virtues of honesty, industry, generosity, humility, chastity and justice.

The apostles too, in the ethical sections of their letters, lay great stress on social righteousness. They portray what should be the mutual relations between husband and wife, parents and children, employers and employees. Paul exposes the gravity of tolerating in the Christian community such sins as factions due to a personality cult, litigation and immorality. The liar is to learn to speak the truth, and the thief to earn his own living so that he can give to those in need. All bitterness, anger, slander and malice are to be put away. Christians are to be kind, tender-hearted, forbearing, tolerant, and even (as Jesus taught) to love and serve their enemies. James inveighs against class distinctions in the Christian fellowship, against our unruly tongues, and against jealousy and selfish ambition. In the last chapter of his letter he sounds just like an Old Testament prophet as he condemns the rich for their luxurious living and their fraudulent treatment of their own farm labourers.

It is true that there are many complex ethical questions of the modern world on which Scripture does not directly pronounce. But the principles are there on which we must form a responsible Christian judgment. Whether the issue is war or violent revolution, pollution, pornography or poverty, or political and economic theory, we cannot escape the labour—and sometimes the pain—of seeking to formulate a Biblically-conditioned Christian opinion.

Witness

The fifth mark of a Christian who 'does' God's word is witness. For truth cannot be concealed or monopolized. If our eyes have been opened to receive it, we know ourselves under compulsion to pass it on. We are 'stewards of the mysteries of God',[35] trustees of His secrets. Not only must we bear witness to the Christ we have come to know, but we cannot bear witness without this knowledge.

The words 'witness' and 'testimony' have been much devalued, and are sometimes employed to describe what is little more than an essay in religious autobiography.

251

But Christian witness is witness to Christ. And the Christ to whom we have a responsibility to witness is not merely the Christ of our personal experience, but the historic Christ, the Christ of the apostolic testimony. There is no other Christ. So if Scripture leads to witness, witness also depends on Scripture.

The Bible, then, has an essential place in the life of a Christian. For the revelation of God leads to worship, the warnings of God to repentance, the promises of God to faith, the commands of God to obedience and the truth of God to witness. It is no exaggeration to say that without Scripture a Christian life is impossible. True, there are still many in the world who are illiterate, and cannot read the Bible. Others can read, but do not or not much, either because of their cultural background or because of the electronic revolution or because of some innate reluctance. Is a Christian life to be denied to them? No, of course not. If (for whatever reason) they do not read Scripture and meditate on it by themselves, I am bound to say I think they will be spiritually impoverished. But they can certainly receive God's word in other ways as I have indicated earlier—through sermons, through group study, through the mass media and through person-to-person communication.

Nevertheless, God's word is indispensable to us, by whatever means we receive it. Jesus Himself put this beyond question when He quoted from Deuteronomy:

'Man shall not live by bread alone, but by every word that proceeds from the mouth of God.'[36]

God's word is as essential to us spiritually as food is to us physically. Both life and health are—quite literally—impossible without it. It is by His word that God implants spiritual life within us.[37] It is by the same word that He instructs, reforms, nourishes, encourages and strengthens us. It is truly by His word alone that the man of God grows into maturity and becomes 'equipped for every good work'.[38]

For Further Reading

Obeying God's Word (1955) and *Expounding God's Word* (1960) by Alan M. Stibbs (IVF, 79 and 112 pages respectively). These two paperbacks form a trilogy with *Understanding God's Word*, which was mentioned at the end of the previous chapter. The first presses upon the reader 'the practical authority of the Word of God' and challenges him to a life of obedient discipleship. The second aims 'to indicate and illustrate some principles and methods of Biblical exposition'. Both books are full of rich examples which demonstrate how to understand and apply the Biblical message.

Holiness by J. C. Ryle (James Clarke edition 1952, 333 pages). John Charles Ryle, the first and evangelical bishop of Liverpool at the end of the last century, brought together in this volume twenty papers on practical, scriptural holiness, 'its nature, hindrances, difficulties and roots'. He was deeply concerned by what he regarded as the unscriptural notions popular in his day, and pleads here for an informed, balanced, wholehearted response to the teaching of Scripture. A spiritual classic which, in my judgment, all Christians should read and absorb.

Learning to Use Your Bible by Oscar E. Feucht (Concordia 1970, 177 pages). The author is an American Lutheran who has had wide experience in both parish ministry and Christian education. The first half of his book contains a fund of practical advice about reading and studying the Bible, both alone and with others. The second half gives information about the Bible's nature, interpretation and contents. It ends with 'thumbnail sketches' of all the Biblical books, and a chart of the Old Testament.

NOTES

1 Ps. 119.105 c.f. 2 Pet. 1.19
2 Ps. 119.24, 30; Ps. 19.7
3 Ps. 95.7
4 Is. 66.2, 5; Ezra 9.4
5 Ps. 19.10; 119.103, 127
6 Ps. 119.162; 1 Pet. 2.2
7 e.g. Jer. 17.23; 18.12; 19.15
8 Jer. 36.21–23
9 Jn. 12.47, 48
10 Mt. 7.24–27
11 Lk. 9.44
12 Ps. 1.1, 2; Ps. 119.97; Josh. 1.8
13 Jer. 5.30, 31
14 Jn. 13.17
15 e.g. 1 Jn. 1.6 literally
16 Js. 1.22
17 Ps. 148.13
18 cf. Neh. 8.8; 1 Tim. 4.13
19 1 Jn. 5.14; Jn. 15.7
20 Js. 1.23–25
21 Eph. 6.17; Heb. 4.12; Acts 2.37
22 Jer. 23.29
23 Jer. 7.3; Is. 1.16, 18
24 Heb. 11.6
25 Heb. 6.12
26 Ps. 9.10
27 2 Pet. 1.4
28 2 Cor. 1.20
29 Rom. 4.21
30 Rom. 10.17
31 Rom. 15.4
32 Jn. 14. 15, 21, 23, 24
33 cf. 1 Thess. 4.1
34 1 Cor. 4.6
35 1 Cor. 4.1
36 Mt. 4.4 quoting Deut. 8.3
37 Js. 1.21; 1 Pet. 1.23–25
38 2 Tim. 3.17